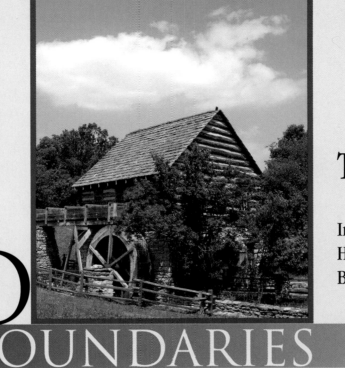

No BOUNDARIES

Table of Contents

Acknowledgments

I don't know how I would ever get through a book without the people who help me by testing patterns, listening to my crazy ideas, critiquing, laughing with me (maybe it's really at me) and those that go the extra mile by doing not one pattern but two or three.

Many thanks go to my wonderful friends who tested the patterns and the "No Boundaries" method: Margaret Falen, Grain Valley; Corky and Peggy Hutinett, Raytown; Rita Briner, Quilter's Station, Lee's Summit; Carol Christopher, Blue Springs; Jackie Howell, Buckner; and Linda Kriesel, Dee Clevenger, Judy Lovell, Clara Diaz, Judy Hill and Brenda Butcher, all of Independence, Missouri.

I really appreciate Norma Phillips of Parkville, Missouri, for letting me bounce ideas off of her when I went brain dead. Bless Karlene Cooper of Kansas City, Missouri, for letting us all gather at her home to sew time and time again.

Thanks to the photographers, Rebecca Friend-Jimenez and Krissy Krauser of the Kansas City Star for the lovely pictures. Thanks to Jo Ann Groves for all her help with the imaging. Thanks also to Cheryl Davis, c davis creative, for her hard work at making these pages look so nice.

We photographed the quilts at a great park in Kansas City, Missouri. It is called The Shoal Creek Living History Museum at 7000 N.E. Barry Road in Kansas City, MO 64156 – Kansas City Missouri Parks and Recreation in Partnership with Shoal Creek Association. Sharon Sumner, president of the Shoal Creek Association, graciously stayed with us even though we were out there on the hottest day of the year.

I want to thank Nedra Forbes for the great job she did quilting most of the quilts. Nedra has her own business called Nedra Quilts in Liberty, Missouri 64068. You may phone Nedra at 816-781-0182 for an appointment.

As always, thanks to Doug Weaver for having so much faith in me.

NO BOUNDARIES

This is a book about quilts, but maybe it's just a tad more than being about quilts. It's also about a concept, an idea. This is an exercise in letting your imagination run wild and not letting your block choice define what fabric you use.

This is about defying tradition, yet incorporating traditional patterns and giving them a fresh, new look. It shows you how to use those wonderful large prints and novelty prints that look so good on the shelf at your favorite quilt shop—you know, those fabrics you leave at the shop because you don't quite know what to do with them.

While we're looking at the quilting aspect, let's also look at some people who are an inspiration to others. Along with the patterns, you will find vignettes of people who have shown incredible courage, or helped make our lives more comfortable or persevered no matter the obstacles. Criticism, ridicule or traditional morés of society failed to stop them from achieving their goals. For these people, there were no boundaries.

NO BOUNDARIES

Bringing Your Fabric Over The Edge

NO BOUNDARIES

By **Edie McGinnis**

Copy Editor: Judy Pearlstein

Photography: Krissy Krauser and Rebecca Friend-Jimenez

Production Assistant: Jo Ann Groves

Book Design: Cheryl Davis, *c davis creative*

Published by KANSAS CITY STAR BOOKS
1729 Grand Boulevard
Kansas City, Missouri 64108

Copyright © 2004 The Kansas City Star Company

First Edition
ISBN 0-9754804-0-5

Printed in the United States of America
by Walsworth Publishing Co.

To order copies, call StarInfo 816.234.4636

www.TheKansasCityStore.com

www.PickleDish.com

About the Author...

Edie McGinnis has been quilting for almost 30 years. She is a member of the American Quilter's Society and the Quilter's Guild of Greater Kansas City. This is the 7th quilt book she has written about *The Kansas City Star* quilt patterns. She teaches quilting classes and gives lectures about *The Star* quilt patterns. She also writes a monthly column for PickleDish.com.

Dedication — to my family, Casey and Courtney McGinnis, Michael and Sarah McGinnis, and Joe McGinnis, your mama loves you.

Bringing Your Fabric Over The Edge

HOW TO BEGIN
the "no boundaries" technique...

NO BOUNDARIES

We choose our fabric for our quilts with the idea that we are going to chop it up into little pieces, then sew them all back together again and get a new look we love. We combine different values of light, medium and dark and we make stunning quilts.

There are fabrics quilters tend to avoid no matter how much we may enjoy the look because the print contains large motifs, animals or people. After all, it is rather disconcerting to see a cat, a dog or a person with its head chopped off. We cannot make our mind's eye finish out those images that are missing a head and it makes us feel uncomfortable. We wander away from that particular fabric even though it may be a wonderful piece.

Let's just do a little thinking in a different direction for a few moments. I call this exercise, "suppose I . . ." For example, "Suppose I refuse to let my block pattern or size define what type of fabric I can use." Or, "Suppose I refuse to cut off that dog's head or that cat's behind." Or, "Suppose I cannot justify chopping off that particular person's head." Or "Suppose I really want to use that particular cluster of flowers rather than cutting it off."

Hmmmmm, what to do, what to do. Let's take a look at the fabrics shown in Figure 1. All work nicely in quilts shown in this book.

Figure 1.

The fabric on the right in *Fig. 1.* on the previous page, *Jungle Song*, was designed by Laurel Burch for Clothworks™. As you can see, the print is large and striking. What a wonderful quilt one could make for anyone who enjoys bright colors and those great animals. This does pose the question though, "How can we use this fabric in a quilt without destroying the integrity of the design?"

Instead of saying, "Suppose...," I will now change that to "I propose." I propose we fussy cut the fabric. Let's call our print our focus fabric. Then, let's find a pattern which comes close to the size needed in which our focus fabric will fit.

If we are working with a 12" block and our focus fabric has a design that measures around 9", we must decide if there is an alternative to chopping off the lion's and tiger's heads.

Figure 2.

Let's use *The Kansas City Star* pattern called Picture Frame for this fabric. Picture Frame has a center piece that measures 7" square before seam allowances are added (7" unfinished). We can cut a 7" square and disregard the print and have a block that looks like *Fig. 2.* or we can

Figure 3.

cut a 7" square, fussy cutting around the portions that don't precisely fit into the square and end up with a block that looks like *Fig. 3*. As you can see in the last photo, we end up with a block that is far more fascinating and adds interest to the quilt without losing vital graphics.

Figure 4.

So how do we accomplish this great look? We use a combination of methods consisting of piecing and appliqué. The first step is to cut a piece of template plastic measuring 7" square, *Fig. 4*, (the finished size of our center square) and place that on the area of the fabric you want to emphasize.

Figure 5.

Put a couple of pieces of double-sided sticky tape on the template to hold it in place. Draw around the template on the reverse side of the fabric with a pencil, *Fig. 5*.

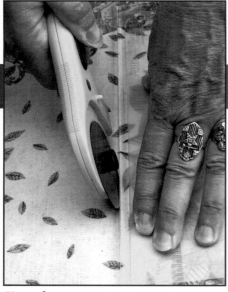

Figure 6.

Figure 7.

Butt an Add-a-Quarter™ ruler against the template. Cut all the **straight** edges, using your rotary cutter, *Fig. 6.*

When you come to a portion of the fabric that you want to keep in the block, but doesn't necessarily fit in the parameters of the template, cut around that portion, using your scissors, adding a $1/8$" – $1/4$" seam allowance, *Fig. 7.* The seam allowance is contingent upon the method you decide to use when you appliqué the pieces in place.

When you are done cutting out your block, it should look like the photo in *Fig. 8.*

I prefer to needle-turn when I appliqué but one can also accomplish this look using any method of appliqué you choose, be it freezer paper appliqué, or satin stitch on the sewing machine or by fusing the pieces in place. When fusing, I recommend you follow the manufacturer's directions and stitch, using a small zigzag, around the edges to reduce the possibility of the piece(s) pulling up or fraying.

Figure 8.

Figure 9.

After cutting out the motifs for the center of the blocks, construct the portions of the block that will go around the center. If using the Picture Frame pattern, you need to make four half-square triangle units and four strip sets for each block, *Fig. 9.* (Complete directions for this block are given on page 66.)

Sew two half-square triangle units to each end of two of the strip

Figure 10.

sets, *Fig. 10.* Sew one strip set to the top of the center piece of the block and then sew the other strip to the bottom of the block. Stop sewing when you reach a point where the print will extend beyond the seam, *Fig. 11.* Backstitch a couple of stitches and skip to the next point to be sewn into the seam line. Every

continued on the next page

Figure 11.

time you reach a point where the print will exceed the seam line, follow the above instructions.

To complete piecing the block, add the two side units that have the half-square triangles included. Again, if you have a portion of the print that exceeds the seam line, stop sewing at that point, backstitch and skip to the next portion to be included in the seam line.

Figure 12.

Press the block after it is pieced together. Pull the portion of the print you want to emphasize out of the seam line to the outside of the block, *Fig. 12*.

Figure 13.

Pin and appliqué the print in place using any method of appliqué you prefer, *Fig. 13*. and *Fig. 14*.

Figure 14.

You will most likely have to clip within one or two threads of the piece you are bringing to the outside of the block,

Fig. 15. After clipping, you should be able to make a sharp turn and have a smooth edge. A little practice goes a long way here.

Figure 15

No matter what pattern you use, the method works the same. As you can see in the Bright Hopes block, one doesn't have to do every block using the "No Boundaries" method. This particular fabric did not require pulling all the butterflies and dragonflies out of the seam line. Some of the motifs fit in the block pattern perfectly without losing parts of the wings or bodies. The larger

butterfly motifs looked better when the wings were appliquéd in place rather than cut off, *Fig. 16*.

Following are fifteen patterns, each included because they work so well

Figure 16.

with the No Boundaries method. Let your imagination fly and use those prints you previously would have reluctantly left behind on your visit to your favorite quilt shop.

Just a Few Hints

All yardage is assuming you have 42" of useable fabric width. This means 42" after you have cut off the selvedges. If your fabric is narrower, you must take that into consideration and buy more. I have attempted to be generous with the fabric requirements without having you buy much more than you need. I do want you to have enough in case of an error though.

Each of the patterns is written for two different quilt sizes. You will find two sets of numbers in the cutting instructions. One set of numbers will be followed by a number in parentheses. The first number indicates the amount of strips, pieces, units, etc., needed for the small quilt. The number in parentheses indicates the amount needed for the large quilt.

If you would like a larger quilt than a size given, add another row of blocks, some sashing, or more borders. Nothing you make has to look exactly like the quilts in this book. Keep in mind that you are free to do as you please. It is, after all, YOUR quilt. Remember that all the blocks in this book are 12" blocks, so if you want to use two different blocks in the same quilt everything should fit together quite nicely.

Choose a focus fabric that has motifs that are a bit larger than the center piece of the block pattern you are using. This way you will have portions of the print to pull out of the seam lines. This book contains patterns that have small, medium and large center pieces so choose a pattern that will be appropriate for your fabric.

I did not give fabric requirements for the binding. So here are a few numbers to remember for that. If you are making straight binding, determine how wide you want the binding to be. Measure the length and the width of the quilt. Add those two numbers together and multiply by 2. Now add an extra 12" to this number and divide by 42. (We are adding the 12" to allow seams for sewing the strips together.) This assumes that you have fabric that is 42" of usable width. Now multiply that number by the width of the strips you are using.

For example: if your quilt is 36" x 40" and you want binding that is 2" before being folded and sewn, you would add 36 + 40 = 76. We would now multiply 76 x 2 = 152 + 12 = 164. Divide this number by 42. 164 ÷ 42 = 3.9 Round that up to 4. Now we know we need 4 strips cut across the width of our fabric. We want each strip to be 2" wide so we will multiply the amount of strips (4) needed by 2 (the width of the strip). 2 x 4 = 8. We need 8" of fabric for the binding.

Each of the quilt patterns are written so they can be strip pieced after "fussy cutting" the center portion of the block from the focus fabric. A few that use oddly shaped pieces recommend using templates.

Templates are provided for people who enjoy using them to check their accuracy and for those of you who like to hand piece. Personally, I love templates. It is so much easier to cut out pieces that are oddly shaped with templates. Following are two methods for using them.

First method:

1. Cut out a template, including seam allowances, using template plastic.

2. Cut a strip across the width of your fabric to straighten it.

3. Measure the height of the template.

4. Using your rotary cutter, cut a strip equal to the height of the template across the fabric.

5. Place the template on the strip.

6. Butt a ruler up to the template, pull the template away and make the cut with your rotary cutter.

7. Replace the template on the strip. Line up the edge of the template with the cut you just made, butt the ruler up to the template, pull the template away and cut the opposing side of the piece.

8. Continue on in this manner until all your pieces are cut.

The next method is done by cutting the template the finished size.

1. Cut a strip across the width of the fabric that measures the size of the template plus $1/2$".

2. Put a piece of double-sided sticky tape on the reverse side of the template. This will hold the template in place.

3. Place the template on the fabric and gently butt an Add-A-Quarter ruler up to the edge of the template and cut, using your rotary cutter.

4. Butt the Add-A-Quarter ruler up against the next edge of the template and cut that side. Continue in this manner until you have cut each side of the desired piece.

5. Move the template and continue cutting until you have gone all the way across the strip of the fabric.

NO BOUNDARIES

Clara Diaz of Independence, Missouri, made this little Attic Windows wall quilt using four blocks. It was quilted by Nedra Forbes of Nedra Quilts, Liberty, Missouri.

ATTIC *windows*

optimism

How can you think of attic windows and not have Anne Frank come to mind?

For 25 months Anne lived above her father's offices in Amsterdam with members of her family and another family of four. After being betrayed to the Nazis, they were sent to Bergen-Belsen. She died of typhus at age 15.

Through her long ordeal, Anne Frank never lost her faith in humanity. A quote from her diary says, "I still believe, in spite of everything, that people are really good at heart." Even though she witnessed the arrests and deportations, she still felt that this evil was something that would eventually pass and peace would again reign.

anne frank

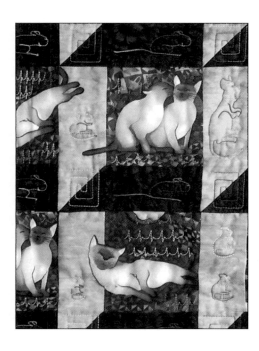

NO BOUNDARIES

ATTIC WINDOWS
12" BLOCK

Fabric needed: Focus fabric, light and dark.

A wall quilt comprised of 12 blocks set three across and four down measures 36" x 48".
Yardage: Focus fabric – Approximately 1 yard*
     Light – $5/8$ yard
     Dark – $5/8$ yard

A large quilt using 56 blocks set seven across and eight down measures 84" x 96".
Yardage: Focus fabric – Approximately 3 $5/8$ yards*
     Light – 2 $3/4$ yards
     Dark – 2 $3/4$ yards

*Check your fabric and see how many motifs you can get from this yardage. You will be using a 4 $1/2$" square so the yardage is dependent upon spacing and repeats of the print.

Cutting instructions:

■ **From the focus fabric** – Cut 48 (224) 4 $1/2$" squares (Template B), being careful to cut around any portion of the print you want to pull out of the seam allowance and emphasize.

■ **From the light fabric** – Cut 8 (38) 2 $1/2$" strips. Subcut each strip into 6 1/2" lengths. *Layer all the pieces right side up.* Place template A on the strip and cut the angle. *All pieces must be cut without the fabric being folded.*

■ **From the dark fabric** – Cut 8 (38) 2 $1/2$" strips. Subcut each strip into 6-1/2" lengths. *Layer all the pieces right side up.* Flip template A over so the reverse side is facing up on the strip and cut the angle. (Flipping the template over gives you template Ar.) *All pieces must be cut without the fabric being folded.*

Piecing instructions:

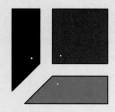

■ This block uses set-in seams. The easiest way to piece this is to put a dot at the quarter inch mark from the edge of each piece that meets at the corner on the wrong side of the fabric.

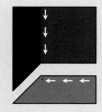

■ Line up the Ar piece, matching the dots and begin sewing at the even edge. Stitch to the dot and stop, then backstitch a couple of

stitches. Add the A piece next and sew until you hit the dot and backstitch. Be careful when sewing on these pieces that you do not run over the portions you want to pull out of the seam line.

■ Fold the block with the right sides together. Put your needle down exactly in the dot where you quit sewing and sew your angled seam closed.

■ Open the unit and press. The unit should look like this.

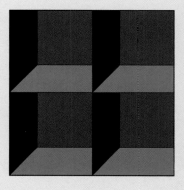

■ Four of these units comprise one block.

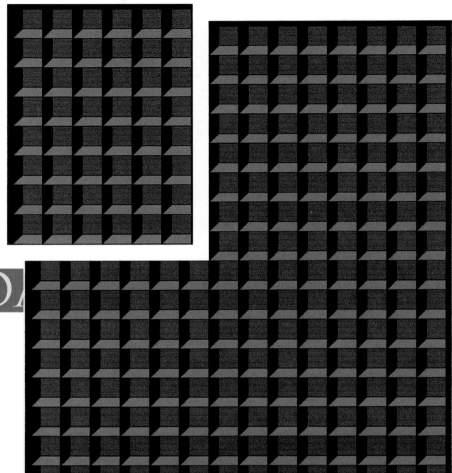

Assembling the Quilt:

■ Sew the blocks together.

■ Layer the top with the batting and the backing and quilt. I did not add a border because this quilt looks pretty cool without one.

ATTIC WINDOWS

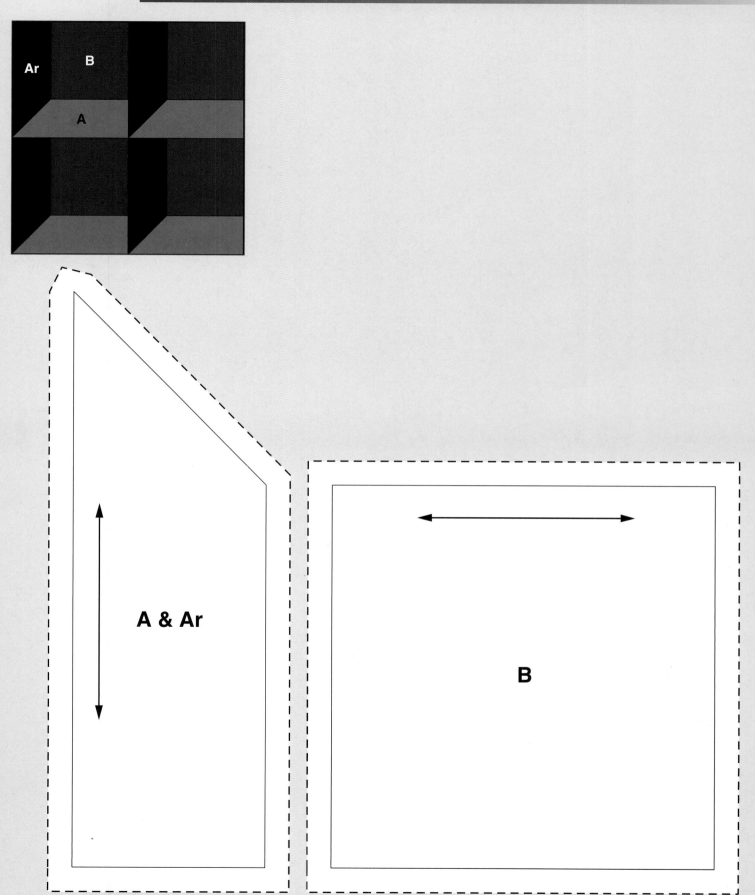

Ar **B**

A

A & Ar

B

The Bright Hopes lap quilt was made by Peggy Hutinett of Raytown, Missouri. Her husband, Corky cuts all her fabric and is an excellent quilter in his own right.

BRIGHT *hopes*

brilliance

The Wizard of Menlo Park was the moniker given to Thomas A. Edison. When Edison was born in 1847, electricity certainly had not reached its full potential. Only after Edison invented the incandescent light bulb in 1879 did cities begin to light up all over the United States.

When Edison was 14 years old, he contracted scarlet fever. The disease presented a new challenge. He became extremely hard of hearing. Never one to be limited, Edison pressed on with determination. By the time he died, he had no less than 1,093 patents in his name. Not only did Edison light up our homes with electricity, he also gave us the phonograph and the first movie camera. That phrase we hear from Hollywood, "Lights! Camera! Action!"

could have been Edison's personal motto.

thomas edison

NO BOUNDARIES

BRIGHT HOPES
12" BLOCK

Fabric needed: Focus fabric, light, medium light, medium and dark.

A crib or wall sized quilt measuring 38" x 50" contains 12 blocks set three across and four down with a 1" finished framing border.

Yardage: Focus fabric – Approximately $1/3$ yard*   Medium – $1/2$ yard
    Light – $1/2$ yard   Dark – $1/2$ yard
    Medium light – $1/2$ yard   Border – $1/4$ yard

A large quilt measuring 74" x 86" requires 42 blocks set six across and seven down with a 1" finished framing border.

Yardage: Focus fabric – Approximately 1 yard*   Medium – 1 $1/2$ yards
    Light – 1 $1/2$ yards   Dark – 1 $1/2$ yards
    Medium light – 1 $1/2$ yards   Border – $1/2$ yard

* Check your focus fabric to make sure you can get the required number of motifs needed for the quilt out of this measurement. The yardage is dependent upon the spacing of the motifs and the repeat.

Cutting instructions:

■ **From the focus fabric** – Cut 48 (168) 2 $\frac{1}{2}$" squares (Template B), being careful to cut around the portion of the motif you want to pull out of the seam allowance.

■ **From the light, medium light, medium and dark fabrics** Cut 6 (19) 2 $\frac{1}{2}$" strips across the width of the fabrics. Subcut the strips into 4 $\frac{1}{2}$" lengths (Template A). You should end up with 48 (168) strips of each color.

Piecing instructions:

Making this block uses a method called **partial seaming**. (Don't freak out on me here because it's really easy. It will feel like you are going backwards if you are right handed.)

■ Begin by sewing the darkest strip to the left side of the center square. As you add each strip, be careful not to run over the portion of the print you want to pull out of the seam line. Sew to within about an inch of the bottom of the square, leaving the rest of the seam open.

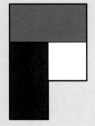

■ Now add the medium strip to the top of the square.

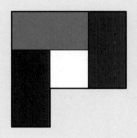

■ Next add the medium light strip to the right side of the square.

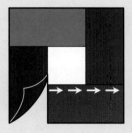

■ Now add the light strip to the bottom of the square pushing the part of the dark strip that is still dangling free out of your way.

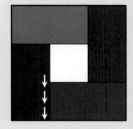

■ Go back to the dark strip now and close the seam line.

■ Pull the portion out of the seam lines you want to emphasize and appliqué in place. Make three more of these units.

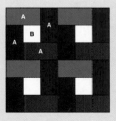

■ Sew the four units together to make one block as shown above. (See quilt assembly on the next page.)

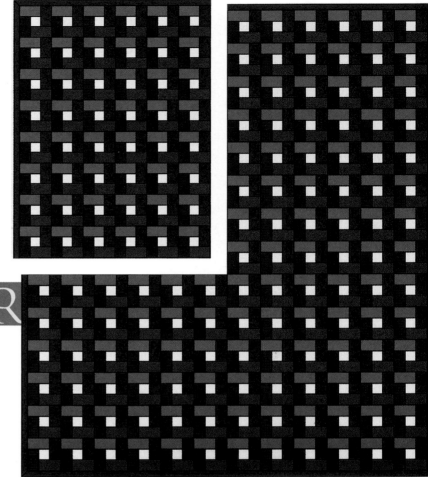

Assembling the Quilt:

■ Sew the blocks together.

■ Measure the quilt through the center of the quilt from top to bottom. Sew enough $1^1/2$" strips together to equal this measurement.

■ Sew the strips to the sides of the quilt.

■ Remeasure the quilt through the center from side to side. Sew enough strips together to equal this measurement and add those to the top and bottom of the quilt.

■ Layer the top of the quilt with batting and backing. Baste and quilt.

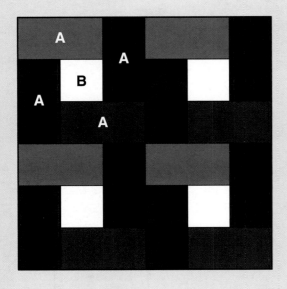

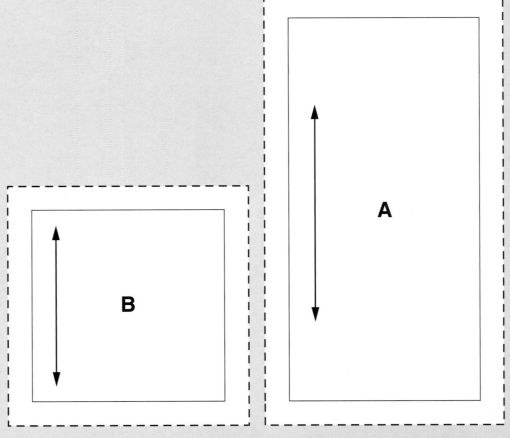

Bright Hopes Variation pieced and appliquéd by Margaret Falen of Grain Valley, Missouri, and quilted by Nedra Forbes of Liberty, Missouri. Margaret made the three-dimensional butterflies by cutting out two butterflies and fusing them together. She then zigzagged around the edges. The butterflies were appliquéd after the quilt was quilted.

BRIGHT *hopes* *variation*

heart

Rosa Parks climbed on a city bus weary from her day's work as a seamstress. She sat down in a seat that was towards the center of the bus. As the bus became close to full, the driver asked Ms. Parks to move to the back. She refused. The bus driver became angry and went for the police and Rosa Parks was arrested for not obeying the segregation laws of Alabama.

When you think one person cannot change the world, think about Rosa Parks. Not only was she tired from her long day of work, but she was tired of oppression and foolish laws enacted because of the color of her skin.

rosa parks

NO BOUNDARIES

**BRIGHT HOPES
VARIATION
12" BLOCK**

Fabric needed: Focus fabric, light, medium light, medium and dark.

A lap quilt using 12 blocks set three across and four down measures 40" x 52" with a 2" finished framing border.
Yardage: Focus fabric – Approximately $1/2$ yard*
      Light – $1/3$ yard
      Medium light – $1/3$ yard
      Medium – $1/3$ yard
      Dark – $3/4$ yard (includes border fabric)

A large quilt using 42 blocks set 6 across and 7 down measures 76" x 88" with a 2" finished framing border.
Yardage: Focus fabric – Approximately 1 $1/2$ yards*
      Light – 1 $1/3$ yards
      Medium light – 1 $1/3$ yards
      Medium – 1 $1/3$ yards
      Dark – 2 yards (includes border fabric)

*Check your focus fabric to make sure you can get the required number of motifs needed for the quilt out of this measurement. The yardage is dependent upon the spacing of the motifs and the repeat.

Cutting instructions:

■ **From the focus fabric** – Cut 12 (42) 6 $\frac{1}{2}$" squares (Template B), being careful to cut around the portion of the print you want to pull out of the seam line and emphasize.

■ **From the four remaining fabrics** – Cut 12 (42) 3 $\frac{1}{2}$" strips across the width of the fabric. Subcut each strip into 9 $\frac{1}{2}$" rectangles (Template A). You should get 4 rectangles per strip.

■ **From the remaining dark fabric** – Cut 2 $\frac{1}{2}$" strips for the framing border.

Piecing instructions:

Making this block uses a method called partial seaming. (It will feel like you are going backwards if you are right handed.)

■ Begin by sewing the medium strip to the left side of the center square. As you add each strip, be careful not to run over the portion of the print you want to pull out of the seam line. Sew to within about an inch of the bottom of the square, leaving the rest of the seam open.

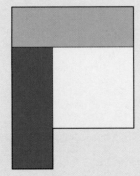

■ Now add the medium light strip to the top of the square.

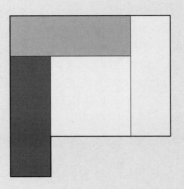

■ Next add the light strip to the right side of the square.

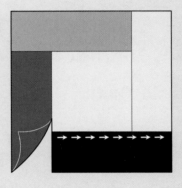

■ Now add the dark strip to the bottom of the square, pushing the part of the medium strip that is still dangling free out of your way.

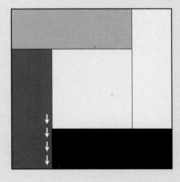

■ Go back to the medium strip now and close the seam line.

■ Pull the portion you want to emphasize out of the seam lines and appliqué in place to complete the block.

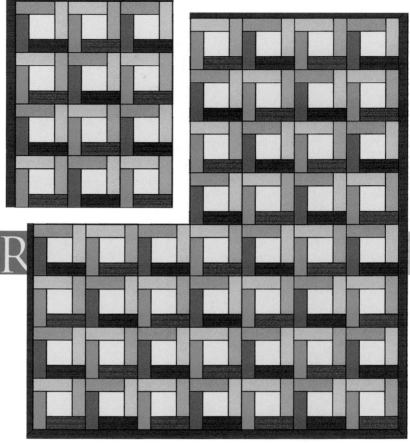

Assembling the Quilt:

■ Sew the blocks together.

■ Measure the quilt through the center of the quilt from top to bottom. Sew enough 2 $^1/_2$" strips together to equal this measurement.

■ Sew the strips to the sides of the quilt. Remeasure the quilt through the center from side to side. Sew enough strips together to equal this measurement and add those to the top and bottom of the quilt.

■ Layer the top of the quilt with batting and backing. Baste and quilt.

BRIGHT HOPES
variation

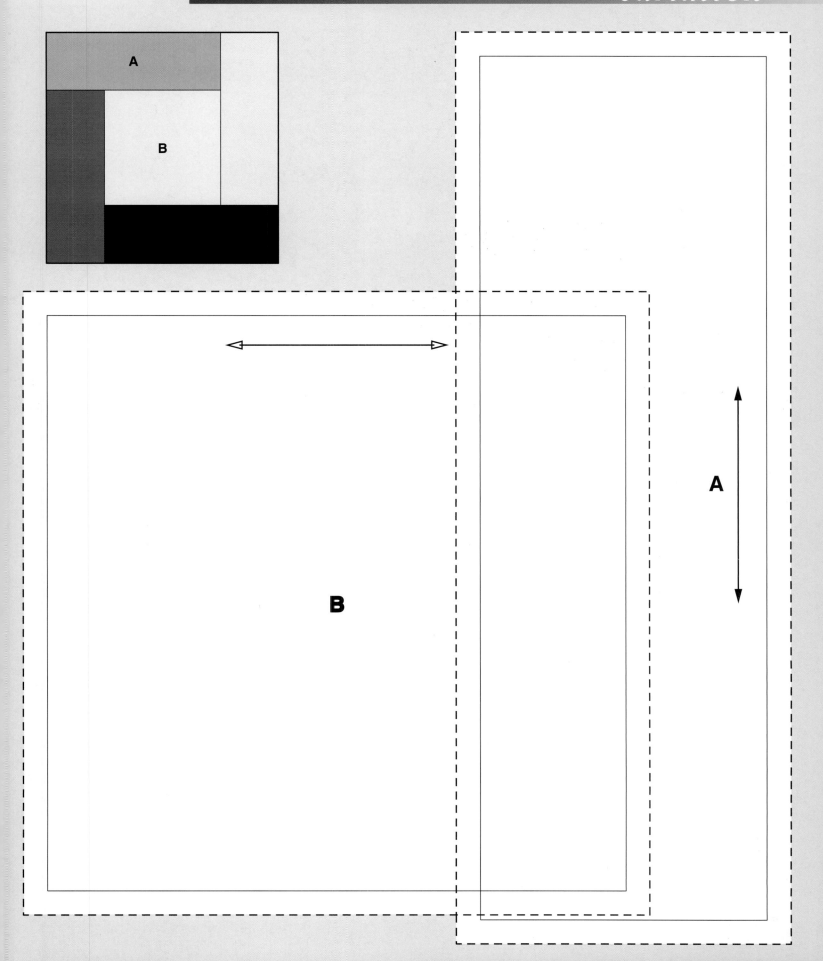

Crow's Nest table runner pieced and appliquéd by Carol Christopher, Blue Springs, Missouri.

CROW'S *nest*

bravery

Christopher Columbus is credited with discovering America. Even though there is some question about that, one has to honor him for his courage. He ventured forth in a time of great superstition with adventure in his soul.

The world was convinced the earth was flat but Columbus took his chances, undeterred by the naysayers who thought he would sail off of the edge.

Think of what it must have been like, after many months on the ocean, to hear the voice crying from the crow's nest, "Land Ho!"

christopher columbus

NO BOUNDARIES

CROW'S NEST
12" BLOCK

Fabric needed: Focus fabric, light, medium, dark and a border fabric.

A lap quilt is made up of twelve blocks set three across and four down and measures 45" x 59". The blocks are sashed with 2" x 12" finished strips and have 2" finished cornerstones. A 2 ^{1}/2" finished framing border completes the quilt.

Yardage: Focus fabric – Approximately ^{1}/2 yard*   Dark – 1 yard
        Light – 1 ^{1}/4 yards   Border – ^{1}/2 yard
        Medium – ^{3}/4 yard

A large quilt made using 42 blocks and sashed with 2" x 12" finished strips and 2" finished cornerstones measures 87" x 101" including a 2 ^{1}/2" finished framing border.

Yardage: Focus fabric – Approximately 1 ^{1}/4 yards*   Dark – 2 ^{3}/4 yards
        Light – 4 yards   Border – 1 yard
        Medium – 1 ^{3}/4 yards

*Check your fabric and see how many motifs you can get from this yardage. You will be using a 4 1/2" square so the yardage is dependent upon spacing and repeats of the print.

CROW'S NEST

Cutting instructions:

■ **From the focus fabric** – Cut 12 (42) 4 $1/2$" squares (Template C), being careful to cut around any portion of the print you want to pull out of the seam line and emphasize.

■ **From the light fabric** – Cut 3 (11) 4 $7/8$" strips across the width of the fabric. Subcut the strips into 4 $7/8$" squares. You will also need to cut 12 (38) 1 $7/8$" strips across the width of the fabric and 1 (2) 2 $1/2$" strip across the width of the fabric. Subcut this (these) strips into 2 $1/2$" squares for the cornerstones in the sashing.

■ **From the medium fabric** – Cut 6 (24) 2 $1/2$" strips across the width of the fabric. Subcut the strips into 12 $1/2$" rectangles.

■ **From the dark fabric** – Cut 3 (11) – 4 $7/8$" strips across the width of the fabric. Also, cut 6 (19) 1 $7/8$" strips across the width of the fabric.

Piecing instructions:

■ You will need to make 48 (168) half-square triangles using the light and dark 4 $7/8$" squares. To make these units, draw a line on the reverse side of the light squares from corner to corner at a 45 degree angle. Place each light square atop a dark square and sew $1/4$" on either side of the line. After you have finished sewing, cut along the line using your rotary cutter. Open each half-square triangle unit and press towards the darkest fabric. If you would rather, you may cut individual triangles using template A.

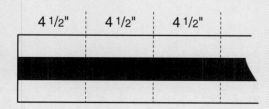

■ You will also need to make bar units. To make the bar units, sew a 1 $7/8$" light strip to either side of a 1 $7/8$" dark strip. Subcut the strip(s) into 4 $1/2$" increments. If you would rather not strip piece, use template B.

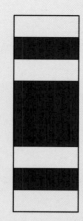

■ To make each block, sew a bar strip to the top and the bottom of the focus fabric square, being careful not to run over the portion of the print you want to emphasize.

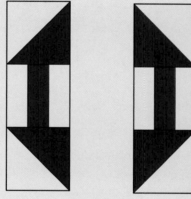

■ Now sew a half-square triangle unit to each end of a bar unit. Make 2 of these units per block. (You need 24 for the small quilt and 84 for the large quilt.)

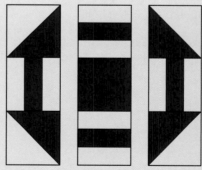

■ Sew the half-square triangle/bar unit to either side of the center square, stopping where necessary so you can pull the portion of the print you want to appliqué to the outside of the block.

■ Pull the portion of the print out of the seam line(s) and appliqué in place to complete the block.

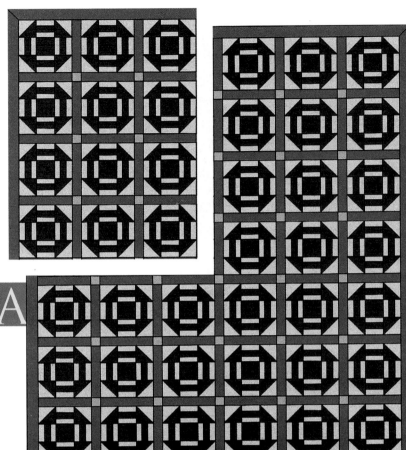

Assembling the Quilt:

■ Sew the blocks together with the sashing and cornerstones.

■ Measure the quilt through the center of the quilt from top to bottom. Sew enough 3" strips together to equal this measurement. Sew the strips to the sides of the quilt.

■ Remeasure the quilt through the center from side to side. Sew enough strips together to equal this measurement and add those to the top and bottom of the quilt.

■ Layer the top of the quilt with batting and backing. Baste and quilt.

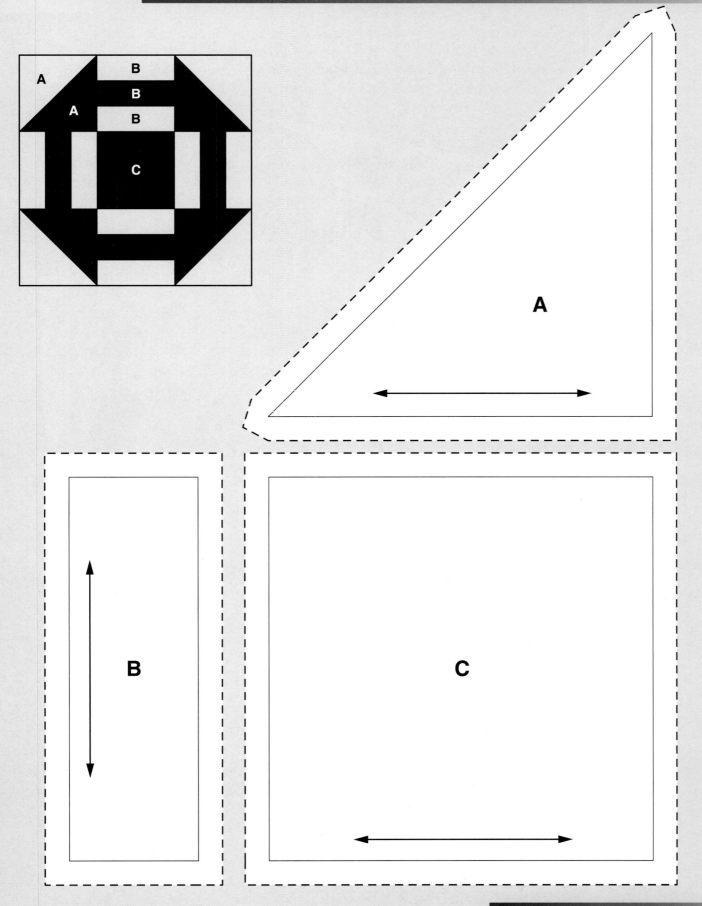

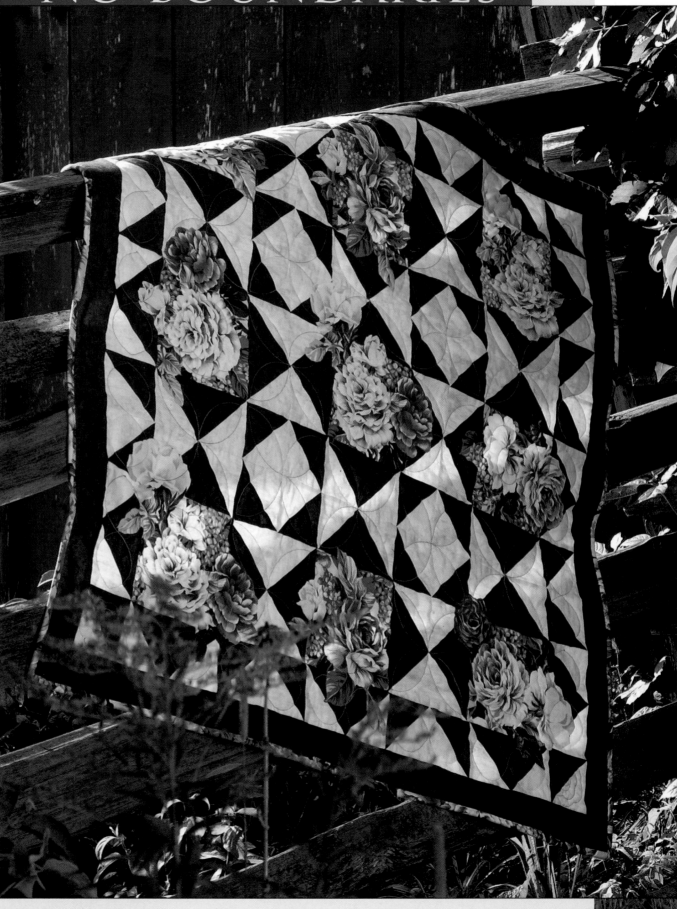

The Cypress quilt was pieced and appliquéd by Judy Hill of Independence, Missouri. It was quilted by Nedra Forbes of Nedra Quilts, Liberty, Missouri.

CYPRESS

beauty

Best known for his poem, "Trees," Joyce Kilmer died at the age of 31. He was a family man and was on the staff of *The New York Times*. Even though he was not required to serve, he enlisted in the New York National Guard. He was sent to France where he was killed by a sniper. Kilmer was awarded the French Croix de Guerre for bravery.

In the mountains of Graham County, North Carolina, lies one of the few remaining stands of virgin hardwood forests. In July of 1936, forestry officials set aside the 3800 acres they had purchased for $28.00 per acre as a living memorial to Kilmer.

Although his life was cut tragically short, Kilmer has been an inspiration to conservationists. In the swamps of Georgia and in the Cache River Basin in Southern Illinois, stand cypress trees as much as 1000 years old. In California, redwoods reign. In the Joyce Kilmer National Forest, poplars tower. Each tree is a treasure, as we are so poignantly reminded by Kilmer's poem.

joyce kilmer

NO BOUNDARIES

CYPRESS
12" BLOCK

Fabric needed: Focus fabric, light, medium, dark and border.

A wall quilt measuring 40" x 40" uses nine blocks set three across and three down, with a 2" finished framing border.
Yardage: Focus fabric – Approximately $1/2$ yard*
        Light – $3/4$ yard
        Medium – $1/4$ yard
        Dark – $1/2$ yard
        Border – $1/2$ yard

A large quilt that measures 88" x 100" uses 56 blocks set seven across and eight down with a 2" finished framing border.
Yardage: Focus fabric – Approximately 2 yards*
        Light – 3 $7/8$ yards
        Medium – 1 $1/2$ yards
        Dark – 2 $1/2$ yards
        Border – $2/3$ yards

*Check your fabric and see how many motifs you can get from this yardage. You will be using a 6 1/2" square so the yardage is dependent upon spacing and repeat of the print.

Cutting instructions:

From the focus fabric – Cut 9 (56) 6 1/2" squares (Template B).

From the light fabric – Cut 6 (34) 3 7/8" strips. Subcut the strips into 54 (336) 3 7/8" squares.

From the medium fabric – Cut 2 (12) 3 7/8" strips. Subcut the strips into 18 (112) 3 7/8" squares.

From the dark fabric – Cut 2 (12) 7 1/4" strips. Subcut the strips into 9 (56) 7 1/4" squares. Cut the squares from corner to corner twice, making 36 (224) C triangles.

Piecing instructions:

You will need to make 36 (224) half-square triangles using 18 (112) of the light and medium 3 7/8" squares.

To make the half-square triangle units, draw a line from corner to corner on the reverse side of the light triangles. Place a light square atop a medium square with the right sides facing and sew 1/4" on either side of the line. Cut along the line using your rotary cutter, then open the units and press towards the darkest fabric.

You should have 36 (224) light 3 7/8" squares remaining. Cut these squares from corner to corner at a 45 degree angle. You should now have 72 (448) A triangles. You can, of course, use template A to cut the triangles for the half-square triangles as well as for these.

Sew a light A triangle to either side of a dark C triangle, thus making a flying geese unit. You will need to make 36 (224) of these flying geese units.

■ Now sew a half-square triangle unit to either end of a flying geese unit. Make sure the point of the flying geese unit points AWAY from the center square.

■ You will need 2 of these units per block (a total of 18 for the wall quilt and 112 for the large quilt.).

■ Sew a flying geese unit to the top and bottom of the focus fabric square being careful to skip over the portion of the print you want to pull out of the seam line and emphasize.

■ Now add a flying geese unit that has the half-square triangles sewn to either end. Be careful to skip over the portion of the print you want to pull out of the seam line.

■ Pull the portion of the print out of the seam line and appliqué it in place to complete the block.

Assembling the Quilt:

■ Sew the blocks together.

■ Measure the quilt through the center from top to bottom. Add 2 $1/2$" border strips to the sides to fit that measurement.

■ Now measure through the center and add 2 $1/2$" border strips that equal that measurement.

■ Layer the top with batting and backing.

■ Baste and quilt.

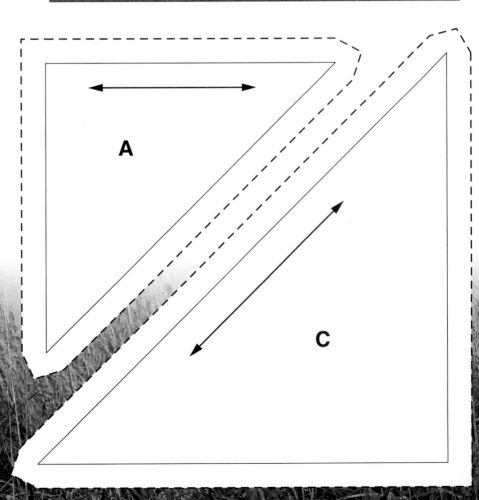

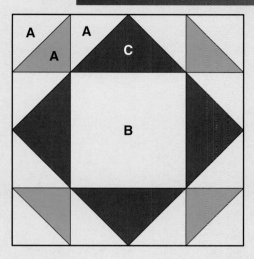

B

NO BOUNDARIES

The Diversion wall quilt was pieced, appliquéd and quilted by Rita Briner, owner of Quilter's Station in Lee's Summit, Missouri.

DIVERSION

humor

Igrew up in an era where a television did not occupy a space in every home. We actually had one but it seldom worked. In my family, diversion was offered through books. Samuel Clemens, known to the world as Mark Twain, was one of my favorite authors.

Those bad boys, Tom Sawyer and Huckleberry Finn, did all the horrible things I wanted to do but didn't have the nerve to implement. I could see the jumping frog from Calaveras County winning just by closing my eyes and using my imagination. I could ride the river boats right along with Twain just by turning the pages of a book.

Mark Twain was more than a writer, he was a story teller. His characters live on, enter-taining us still, even though nearly 100 years have passed since his death.

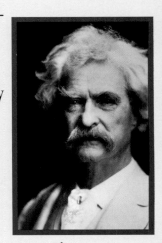

samuel clemens

NO BOUNDARIES

DIVERSION
12" BLOCK

Fabric needed: Focus fabric, light, medium and dark.

A small quilt measuring 43" x 55" is made up of 12 blocks set 3 across and 4 down. It is framed with 2 borders measuring 1" and 2 $1/2$" finished.

Yardage: Focus fabric – Approximately $1/2$ yard*

Light – 1 $1/8$ yards	Dark border – $1/4$ yard
Medium – 1 $1/2$ yards	Medium border – $1/2$ yard

A large quilt measuring 79" x 91" is made up of 42 blocks set 6 across and 7 down. It has two borders measuring 1" and 2 $1/2$" finished.

Yardage: Focus fabric – Approximately 2 yards*

Light – 3 yards	Dark border – $1/2$ yard
Medium – 3 yards	Medium border – 1 yard

*Check your fabric and see how many motifs you can get from this yardage. You will be using a 6 $1/2$" square so the yardage is dependent upon spacing and repeats of the print.

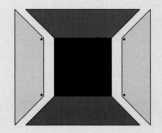

Cutting instructions:

■ **From the focus fabric** – Cut 12 (42) 6 $^1/2$" squares (Template B), being careful to cut around the portions you want to appliqué to the outer edges of the block.

■ **From the medium and light fabrics** – Cut 8 (28) 3 $^1/2$" strips. Subcut the strips into 13 $^1/4$" rectangles. Layer 4 to 8 rectangles atop each other and place template A on the rectangles. Butt a ruler up to the template, pull the template away and cut the angle using your rotary cutter. Repeat for the other angle. You will need 24 (84) light and 24 (84) medium A pieces.

■ **From the dark border fabric** – Cut 5 (9) 1 $^1/2$" strips.

■ **From the medium border fabric** – Cut 5 (9) 3" strips.

Piecing instructions:

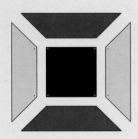

■ Mark a dot $^1/4$" from the edge on each corner of the 6 $^1/2$" square and on each short end of each A piece.

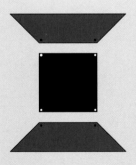

■ Match up the dots on a medium A piece to the dots on the top of the 6 1/2" square. Sew from dot to dot. Now add a medium A piece to the bottom of the square. Again, match up the dots and sew from dot to dot. Be careful not to sew down the portion of the print you will be pulling out of the seam allowance.

■ Add a light A piece to either side of the square and sew from dot to dot. Remember to skip over the portion you will be pulling out of the seam allowance.

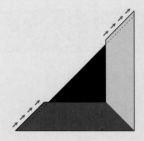

■ Fold the piece at a 45 degree angle and sew two opposing seams closed.

■ Open the block and refold in the opposite direction and sew the other two seams closed.

■ Appliqué the portion of the print you pulled out of the seam line to complete the block.

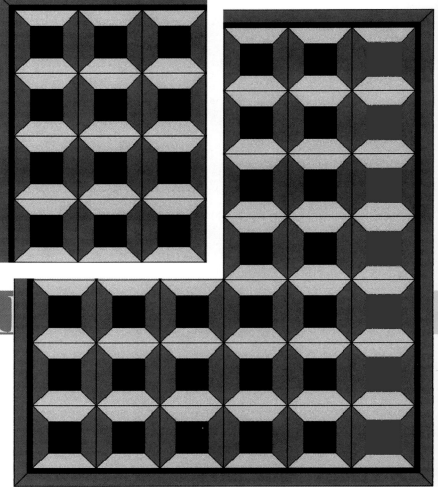

Assembling the Quilt:

■ Sew the blocks together. Measure the quilt through the center from top to bottom. Sew enough 1 $^1/_2$" dark strips together to equal that measurement. Now sew enough 3" medium strips together to equal that measurement.

■ Sew the dark and the medium strips together and sew them to the sides of the quilt.

■ Measure the quilt through the center from side to side. Sew dark strips together to equal that measurement. Sew the same amount of medium strips together.

■ Sew the dark strips to the medium strips. Sew them to the top and bottom of the quilt.

■ Layer the top, backing and batting. Baste and quilt.

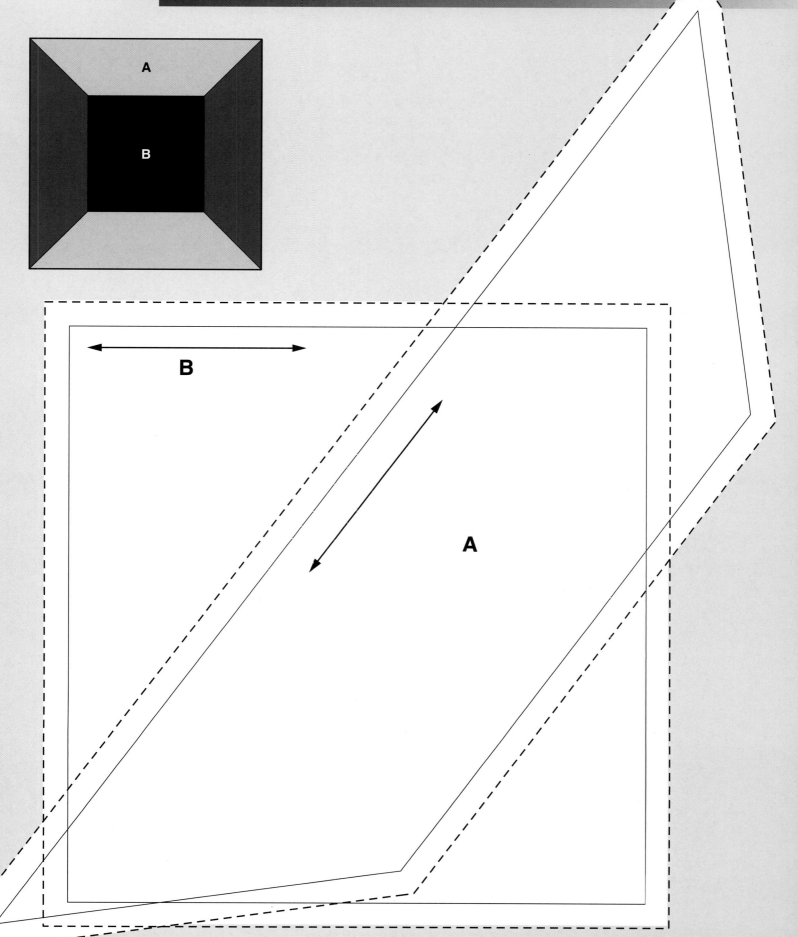

NO BOUNDARIES

The Greek Cross
wall hanging was
pieced and
appliquéd by Jackie
Howell, Buckner,
Missouri. It was
quilted by Nedra
Forbes of Nedra
Quilts, Liberty,
Missouri.

GREEK *cross*

genius

Socrates, Plato, Euclid, Pythagoras and Aristotle, members of an ancient society, passed along their ideas on philosophy, mathematics, ideals and democracy – all being taught in universities to our young people today. These were people far ahead of their time and above the norm in society.

Think about it. Thousands of years have passed and we are still learning from people who lived their lives with none of the advantages we have today. No computers, no calculators, no slide rule – just pure genius.

socrates

NO BOUNDARIES

**GREEK CROSS
12" BLOCK**

Fabric needed: Focus fabric, dark, medium and light.

A wall-hanging measures 41" square and contains nine blocks set three across and three down and has a 2 $^{1}/_{2}$" finished framing border.

Yardage: Focus fabric – Approximately $^{1}/_{4}$ yard*
        Light – $^{1}/_{2}$ yard
        Medium – $^{3}/_{4}$ yard
        Dark – $^{1}/_{3}$ yard
        Border – $^{1}/_{2}$ yard

A large quilt measuring 77" x 89" has 42 blocks set six across and seven down with a 2 $^{1}/_{2}$" finished framing border.

Yardage: Focus fabric – Approximately $^{3}/_{4}$ yard*
        Light – $^{3}/_{4}$ yard
        Medium – 3 $^{1}/_{4}$ yards
        Dark – 1 $^{1}/_{2}$ yards
        Border – $^{7}/_{8}$ yard

*Check your focus fabric to make sure you can get the required number of motifs needed for the quilt out of this measurement. The yardage is dependent upon the spacing of the motifs and the repeat.

Cutting instructions:

From the focus fabric – Cut 9 (42) 4 $^1/_2$" squares (Template C). Be careful to cut around the portion of the print you want to pull out of the seam allowance.

From the light fabric – Cut 3 (11) 4 $^7/_8$" strips across the width of the fabric. Subcut each strip into 4 $^7/_8$" squares. You should have 24 (84) squares.

From the medium fabric – Cut 3 (11) 4 $^7/_8$" strips across the width of the fabric. Subcut each strip into 4 $^7/_8$" squares for a total of 24 (84) squares. Cut 4 (19) 2 $^1/_2$" strips across the width of the fabric.

From the dark fabric – Cut 4 (19) 2 $^1/_2$" strips across the width of the fabric.

From the border fabric – Cut 4 (9) 3" strips.

Piecing instructions:

You will need to make 36 (168) half-square triangle units using the light and medium 4 $^7/_8$" squares you cut. To make the half-square triangles, draw a line from corner to corner on the reverse side of the light squares. Place a light square atop a medium square and sew $^1/_4$" on each side of the line you drew. When you finish sewing, cut along the line with your rotary cutter, open each unit and press the seam towards the darkest fabric. If you wish, rather than strip piecing, you may cut individual triangles using template A.

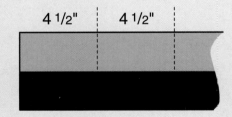

Next you will need to make 36 (168) bar units. To make these, sew the medium and the dark 2 $^1/_2$" strips together. Press the strips with the seam allowance towards the darkest fabric. Subcut the strips into 4 $^1/_2$" lengths. If you would rather not strip piece, use template B.

■ Sew a bar unit to the top and bottom of the 4 $^1/_2$" focus fabric square. Keep the darkest fabric towards the square and be careful to skip over the portion of the print you want to bring out of the seam line.

■ Sew a half-square triangle unit to either side of a bar unit. Watch the color placement of the units. The medium portion of the half square triangles needs to touch the darkest portion of the bar unit as shown in the diagram above.

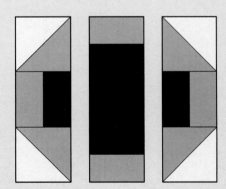

■ You will need two of these units per block. Add one to each side of the center portion of the block. Again, make sure you skip over the portion of the block you want to bring out of the seam line.

■ Bring the portion of the block you want to emphasize out of the seam line and appliqué in place to complete the block.

Assembling the Quilt:

■ Sew the blocks together. Measure the quilt through the center of the quilt from top to bottom. Sew enough 3" strips together to equal this measurement.

■ Sew the strips to the sides of the quilt.

■ Remeasure the quilt through the center from side to side. Sew enough strips together to equal this measurement and add those to the top and bottom of the quilt.

■ Layer the top of the quilt with batting and backing. Baste and quilt.

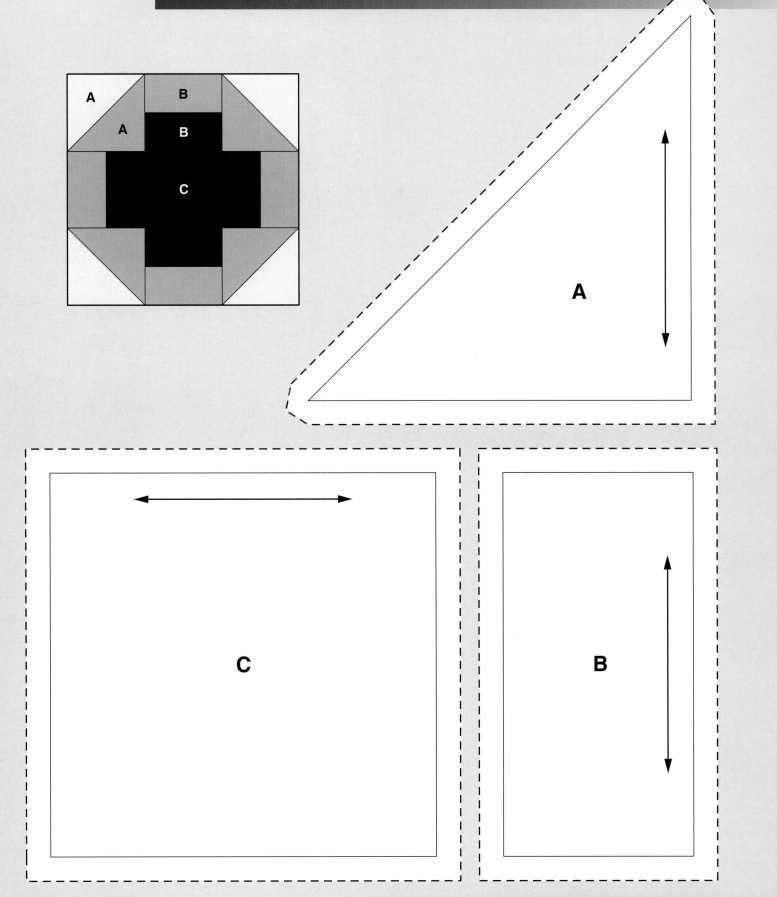

NO BOUNDARIES

The King's Crown wall
quilt was pieced and
appliquéd by Judy Lovell
of Independence,
Missouri. It was quilted
by Nedra Forbes of
Nedra Quilts,
Liberty, Missouri.

KING'S
crown

valor

John Hancock, Thomas Paine, Patrick Henry, Paul Revere, George Washington, patriots all, were determined to free this country from the king's crown. The colonies had been stifled by horrendous taxes imposed by King George. Freedom, representation and democracy were the patriot's dream.

The patriots so believed in their cause that they were willing to give up their lives for their convictions. Patriots step forward in every generation and in every war. Heroes all, they risk their lives for those of us who stay behind.

john hancock

NO BOUNDARIES

KING'S CROWN
12" BLOCK

Fabric needed: Focus fabric, light, medium, medium dark and dark.

A wall quilt measuring 38" square is made up of nine blocks set three across and three down and has a 1" finished framing border.

Yardage: Focus fabric – Approximately 1/2 yard*
    Light – 1/2 yard
    Medium – 1/4 yard

Medium dark – 1/4 yard
Dark – 2/3 yard (includes border fabric)

A large quilt measuring 88" x 100" with a 1" finished framing border is made using 56 blocks. The blocks are set seven across and eight down.

Yardage: Focus fabric – Approximately 1 3/4 yards*
    Light – 2 3/4 yards
    Medium – 1 yard

Medium dark – 1 yard
Dark – 3 yards (includes border fabric)

*Check your fabric and see how many motifs you can get from this yardage. You will be using a 6 1/2" square so the yardage is dependent upon spacing and repeat of the print.

Cutting instructions:

■ **From the focus fabric –** Cut 9 (56) 6 ¹/₂" squares (Template C), being careful to cut around the portion of the print you want to pull out of the seam line and emphasize.

■ **From the light fabric –** Cut 4 (23) 3 ⁷/₈" strips. Subcut the strips into 3 ⁷/₈" squares. Cut each square at a 45 degree angle from corner to corner or use Template B.

■ **From the medium and medium dark fabrics –** Cut 1 (13) 3 ¹/₂" strip across the width of the fabric. Subcut the strip(s) into 3 ¹/₂" A squares.

■ **From the dark fabric –** Cut 2 (12) 7 ¹/₄" strips. Subcut the strips into 7 ¹/₄" squares. Cut each square from corner to corner twice as shown below making the D triangles.

■ Sew a medium dark A square to one end of a flying geese unit then add a medium A square to the other end. Make two of these units per block.

■ Sew a flying geese unit to the top and bottom of the focus fabric square, being careful not to run over the portion of the print you want to bring out of the seam allowance and emphasize.

Piecing instructions:

NOTE: *All flying geese point away from the center!*

■ Sew a light B triangle to either side of the dark D triangle to make flying geese units. You will need 36 (224) flying geese units.

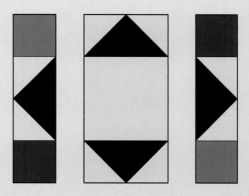

■ Add a flying geese unit (one that already has the squares attached) to either side of the block.

■ Pull the portion of the print you are emphasizing out of the seam line and appliqué it in place to complete the block.

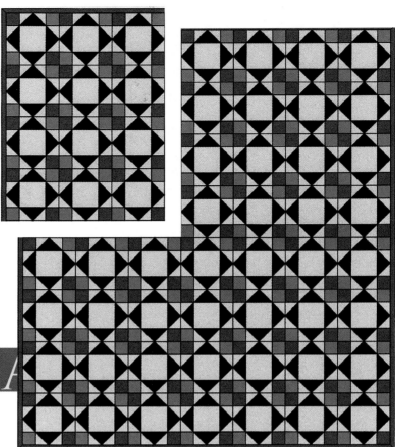

Assembling the Quilt:

■ Sew the blocks together.

■ Measure the quilt through the center of the quilt from top to bottom. Sew enough 1 $\frac{1}{2}$" strips together to equal this measurement.

■ Sew the strips to the sides of the quilt.

■ Remeasure the quilt through the center from side to side. Sew enough strips together to equal this measurement and add those to the top and bottom of the quilt.

■ Layer the top of the quilt with batting and backing. Baste and quilt.

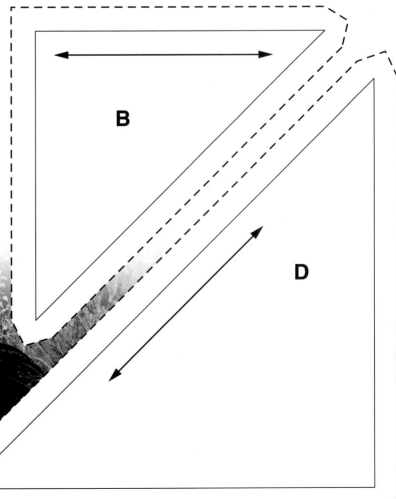

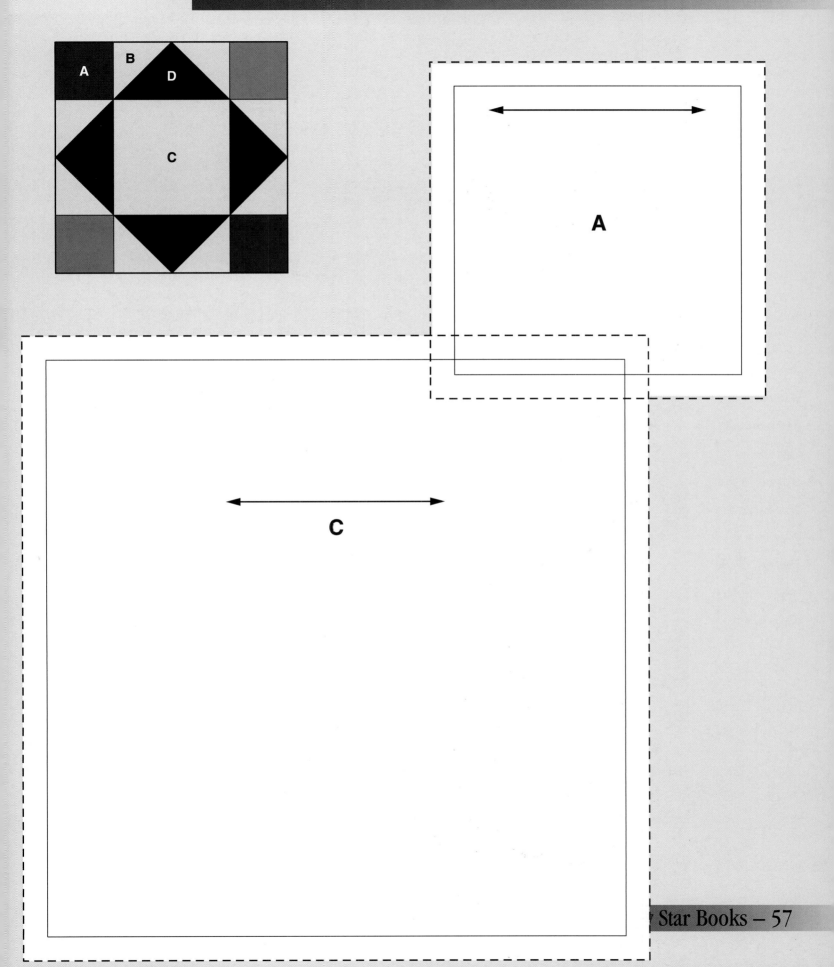

NO BOUNDARIES

The Kitchen Woodbox wall quilt was pieced and appliquéd by Margaret Falen of Grain Valley, Missouri. It was quilted by Nedra Forbes of Nedra Quilts, Liberty, Missouri.

KITCHEN *woodbox*

determination

I was raised on Abraham Lincoln stories, having been born in Central Illinois. No one in my home town of Tremont, Illinois, graduated from grade school without a field trip to Springfield to visit the Lincoln sites and New Salem.

At New Salem, every child who peeped into the doorway of one of those log cabins, was amazed at how small an area Abraham Lincoln lived in. It was easy to picture him, lying on his stomach in front of a blazing fire, reading and scratching out his homework on a slate.

What is not so easy to comprehend is Lincoln's sheer determination. He never realized that he should stay a poor farmer or rail splitter or store clerk. Instead of allowing himself to be held back, he forged on, defying all odds, and became one of  our most beloved presidents.

abraham lincoln

NO BOUNDARIES

KITCHEN WOODBOX
12" BLOCK

Fabric needed: Focus fabric, light, medium and dark.

A small quilt using nine blocks set three across and three down measures 38" x 38". It has a 1" finished framing border.

Yardage: Focus fabric – Approximately $1/2$ yard*

       Light – $2/3$ yard

       Medium – $3/4$ yard

       Dark – $3/4$ yard

       Border – $1/4$ yard

A large quilt set six blocks across and seven blocks down measures 74" x 86" with a 1" finished framing border.

Yardage: Focus fabric – Approximately 1 $1/4$ yards*

       Medium – 3 yards

       Light – 1 $3/4$ yards

       Border – $1/2$ yard

*Check your fabric and see how many motifs you can get from this yardage. You will be using a 4 $1/2$" square so the yardage is dependent upon spacing and repeat of the print.

Cutting instructions:

■ **From the focus fabric** – Cut 9 (42) 4 $1/2$" squares (Template C), being careful to cut around the portion you want to emphasize.

■ **From the light fabric** – Cut 3 (11) 4 $7/8$" strips. Subcut the strips into 4 $7/8$" squares. Cut each square into 2 triangles (Template A).

■ **From the medium and dark fabrics** – Cut 9 (42) 2 $1/2$" strips.

■ **From the border fabric** – Cut 5 (9) 1 $1/2$" strips.

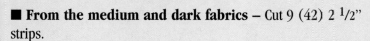

Piecing instructions:

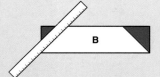 

■ Sew each of the medium and dark strips together using a $1/4$" seam allowance. Before you press the strips open, place template B on the strip. Butt a ruler up to the angled edge of the template. Pull the template away while holding the ruler in place. Cut the angle using your rotary cutter. Reposition the template and cut the other angle using the same technique. Open the piece and press the seam towards the darkest fabric. You will need 36 (168) of these units.

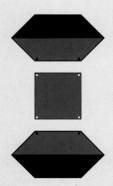

■ On the reverse side of the fabric, mark a dot $1/4$" from the cutting edge on the square and on the lightest side of the B unit. After matching the dots, sew a B strip unit to the top and the bottom of the focus fabric square from dot to dot. Be careful not to run over the portion of the print you want to pull out of the seam allowance.

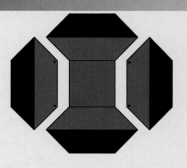

■ Next sew a B unit to each of the remaining sides matching the dots and sewing from dot to dot.

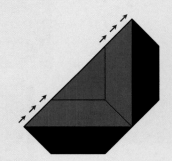

■ Fold the block at a 45 degree angle with the right sides together and close the two angled opposing seams. Open the block and refold it to sew the other two opposing seams.

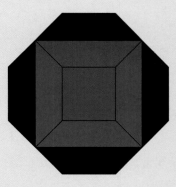

■ Your block should now look like the drawing above.

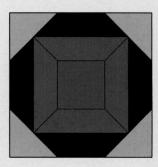

■ Add the light triangles to the corners. Pull the portion of the print you are emphasizing out of the seam line and appliqué in place.

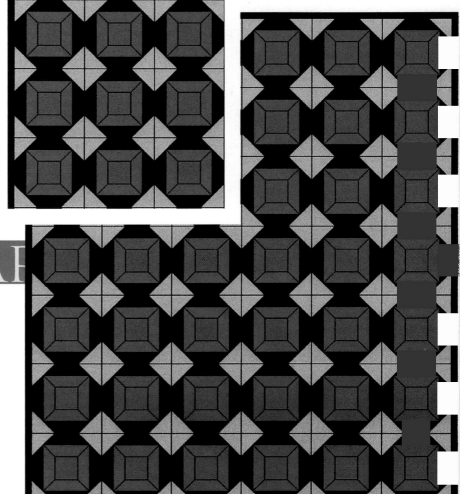

Assembling the Quilt:

■ Sew the blocks together.

■ Measure the quilt through the center from top to bottom. Add border strips to the sides to fit that measurement.

■ Now measure through the center and add border strips that equal that measurement.

■ Layer the top with batting and backing. Baste and quilt.

KITCHEN WOODBOX

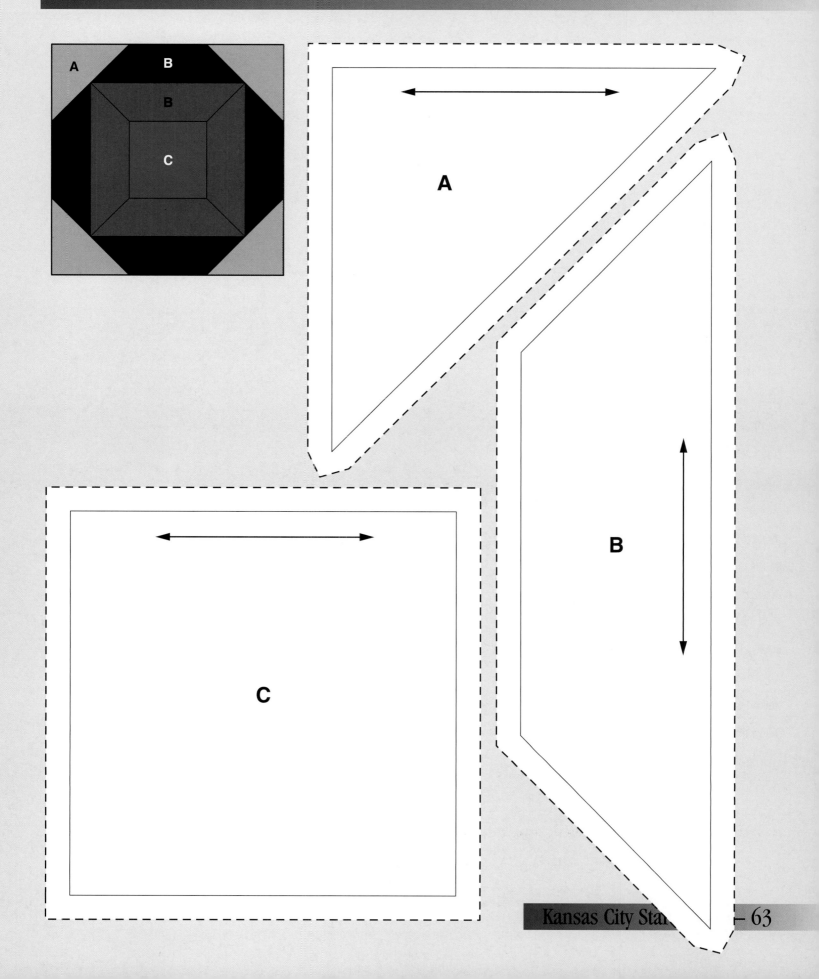

A

B

C

NO BOUNDARIES

The Picture Frame quilt was pieced and appliquéd by Linda Kriesel of Independence, Missouri. Linda chose to use nine blocks in her wall hanging and she used a 2 1/2" border. The quilt was quilted by Nedra Forbes of Nedra Quilts, Liberty, Missouri.

PICTURE *frame*

tenacity

I don't know about you, but I remember the first camera that was used in our house. It was a Brownie and looked like a box. There was a lens in the front of the camera, a button you pushed and a view finder on the top. My sisters and I still have photos of us as small children that had been taken with our Brownie camera.

I expect every family in the United States should be honoring George Eastman this year. This is the 150th anniversary of his birth. Eastman made photography so simple that even the most uninformed individual with no photographic skills whatsoever could still record his surroundings and his life.

According to George Eastman House, it took Eastman three years to develop an easier way to process film – three years of working in his mother's kitchen before he was finally successful. Eastman recognized how cumbersome and unworkable the photographic process was in his time. He also recognized that great improvements could be made and went forth to meet the challenge.

george eastman

PICTURE FRAME
12" BLOCK

Fabric needed: Focus fabric, light and dark.

A small quilt measuring 39" x 51" using 12 blocks is set 3 across and 4 down and uses a 1 $^1/_2$" finished framing border.
Yardage: Focus fabric – Approximately $^2/_3$ yard*
      Light – $^3/_4$ yard
      Dark – 1 yard (includes border)

A large quilt measuring 78" x 90" has 42 blocks set 6 across and 7 down with a 3" finished framing border.
Yardage: Focus fabric – Approximately 2 yards*
      Light – 2 $^1/_2$ yards
      Dark – 3 $^1/_2$ yards (includes border)

*Check your fabric and see how many motifs you can get from this yardage. You will be using a 7 1/2" square so the yardage is dependent upon spacing and repeats of the print.

PICTURE FRAME

Cutting instructions:

From the focus fabric – Cut 12 (42) 7 $1/2$" squares (Template C), being careful to cut around the portions you want to appliqué to the outer edge of the block.

From the light fabric – Cut 2 (7) 3 $3/8$" strips and 10 (34) 1 $3/4$" strips across the width of the fabric. Subcut the 3 $3/8$" strips into 3 $3/8$" squares.

From the dark fabric – Cut 2 (7) 3 $3/8$" strips and 10 (34) 1 $3/4$" strips across the width of the fabric. Subcut the 3 $3/8$" strips into 3 $3/8$" squares.

NOTE: You will be making two different color ways of this block. By alternating the colors, each block will show up after being sewn together thereby creating a more interesting pattern.

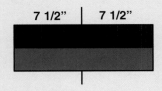

Sew the dark 1 $3/4$" strips to the light 1 $3/4$" strips. Cut each strip into 7 $1/2$" increments. You should have 48 (168) strip units. If you would rather, you may cut each strip using template B.

Now draw a line from corner to corner on the reverse side of each of the 3 $3/8$" squares.

Place each light square atop each dark square with the right sides facing. Sew $1/4$" on each side of the line. Cut on the marked line, open the unit and press towards the darkest fabric. You need 48 (168) half-square triangles. You may also make these by cutting the A triangles individually.

Piecing instructions:

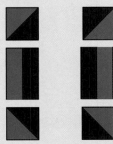

■ Sew a half-square triangle unit to either end of a strip set. The same color of the portion of the strip set that touches the center square should have that color of the half square triangle turned towards the center of the block. See the diagram above. You need 12 (42) of these units. Make 12 (42) units reversing the color order.

■ Sew a strip set to the top and bottom of a 7 $1/2$" focus fabric square, being careful to skip over the portion of the print you want to emphasize.

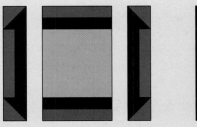 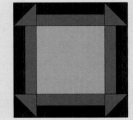

■ Add a half-square triangle/strip set unit to each side of the square.

■ Make half of the blocks with the lighter colored bar and half-square triangles turned toward the center square and half with the darker colored bar and half-square triangles turned towards the center square.

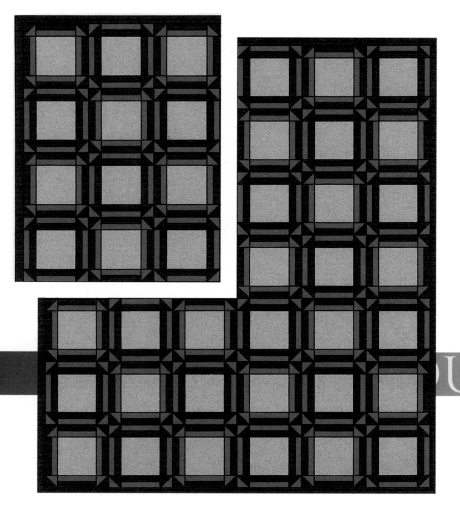

Assembling the Quilt:

■ Sew the blocks together, alternating colors.

■ Measure the quilt through the center of the quilt from top to bottom. Sew enough 2" (3 $\frac{1}{2}$") strips together to equal this measurement.

■ Sew the strips to the sides of the quilt.

■ Remeasure the quilt through the center from side to side. Sew enough strips together to equal this measurement and add those to the top and bottom of the quilt.

■ Layer the top of the quilt with batting and backing.

■ Baste and quilt.

B

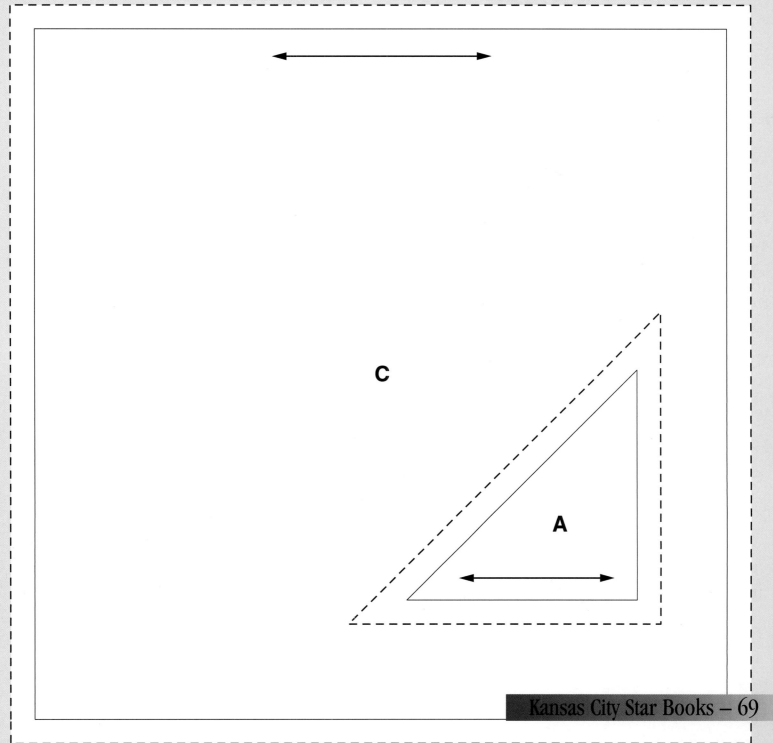

C

A

Dee Clevenger of Independence, Missouri, made the Radio Windmill wall hanging. She chose to use nine blocks. The quilt was quilted by Nedra Forbes of Nedra Quilts, Liberty, Missouri.

RADIO
windmill

vision

Marconi? Tesla? Both are credited with the invention of the radio. After applying for a patent in 1897, Tesla was granted a basic radio patent in 1900. Marconi filed for a patent in 1900 and was turned down repeatedly because of Tesla's prior patents. Marconi persisted with his work and was awarded a patent in 1904 and received the Nobel Prize in 1911.

Things certainly changed since that first signal was received across the Atlantic Ocean in 1901. In the ensuing years, families were entertained with music and stories and were informed of the events of the nation. Even people in rural areas without electricity were able to listen to the radio with the help of the device called the Radio Windmill. The Radio Windmill was a windcharger that would recharge a 6-volt storage battery. Of course you weren't supposed to run the radio and the charger at the same time. You might blow all those glass tubes!

marconi

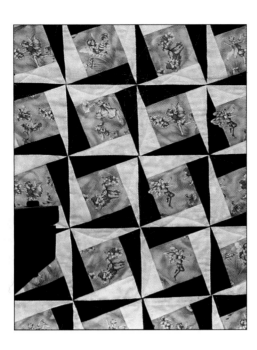

NO BOUNDARIES

RADIO WINDMILL
12" BLOCK

Fabric needed: Focus fabric, light and dark.

A lap quilt that measures 40" x 52" is made using 12 blocks set three across and 4 down and is framed with a 2" border.
Yardage: Focus fabric – Approximately $1/3$ yard*
      Light – 1 $1/4$ yards
      Dark – 1 $3/4$" yards (includes border fabric)

A large quilt measuring 86" x 98" with a 1" framing border uses 48 blocks set seven across and eight down.
Yardage: Focus fabric – Approximately 1 yard*
      Light – 4 $1/2$ yards
      Dark – 5 yards (includes border fabric)

* Check your fabric to see how many motifs you can get from this yardage. You will be using a 4 $1/2$" square so the yardage is dependent upon spacing and repeats of the print.

RADIO WINDMILL

Cutting instructions:

■ **From the focus fabric** – Cut 12 (48) 4 $1/2$" squares (Template B), being careful to cut around each of the portions you want to appliqué to the outer edge of the block.

■ **From the light fabric** – Cut 16 (64) 2 $1/2$" strips across the width of the fabric. Subcut the strips into 96 (384) wedges using template A. **MAKE SURE YOU OPEN EACH STRIP BEFORE LAYERING AND CUTTING. YOU DO NOT WANT MIRROR IMAGES OF THIS PIECE.**

■ **From the dark fabric** – Cut the same amount of wedges. You will have enough fabric left to cut 5 (9) 1 $1/2$" strips across the width of the fabric. **MAKE SURE YOU OPEN EACH STRIP BEFORE LAYERING AND CUTTING. YOU DO NOT WANT MIRROR IMAGES OF THIS PIECE.**

Piecing instructions:

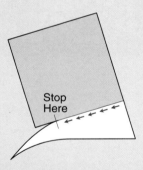

■ Sew a light wedge to the center square, leaving about an inch or so unsewn. Be careful to skip over any portion of the print you want to emphasize by appliquéing to the outer portion of the block.

■ Now add a dark wedge.

■ Sew a light wedge to the top. (It feels like you're doing this backwards, doesn't it!)

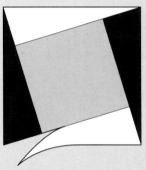

■ Now add the dark wedge to the remaining side of the center square.

■ Go back to the first seam and close it. Four of these units comprise one block. **Since the fabric in the center of the block is directional, you will want to alternate the placement of the light and the dark wedges.** See the piecing diagram on page 75.

■ Pull the portion of the print you want to emphasize out of the seam line(s) and appliqué in place.

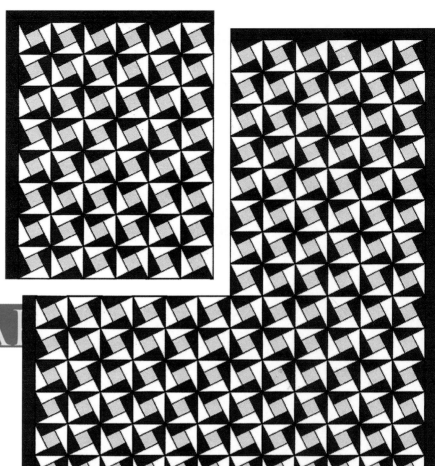

Assembling the Quilt:

■ Measure the quilt through the center of the quilt from top to bottom. Sew enough 1 $\frac{1}{2}$" strips together to equal this measurement. Sew the strips to the sides of the quilt.

■ Remeasure the quilt through the center from side to side. Sew enough strips together to equal this measurement and add those to the top and bottom of the quilt.

■ Layer the top of the quilt with batting and backing.

■ Baste and quilt.

RADIO WINDMILL

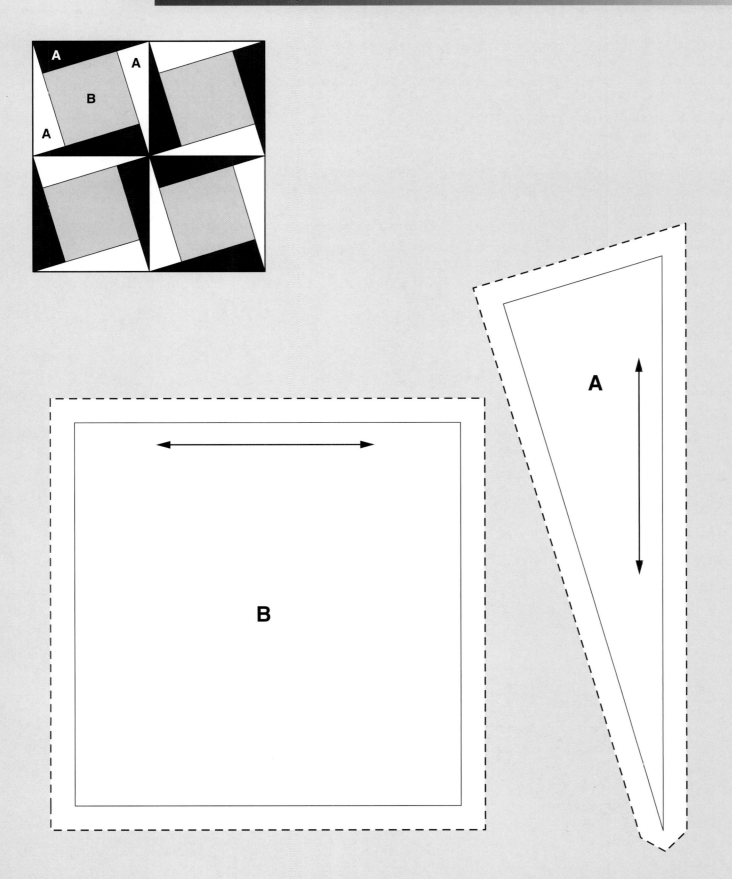

A

B

A

NO BOUNDARIES

The Sheepfold lap quilt was pieced and appliquéd by Brenda Butcher of Independence, Missouri. Nedra Forbes of Nedra Quilts, Liberty, Missouri, quilted it.

SHEEPFOLD

heroism

Gregory Boyington was born on December 4, 1912. Growing up in a broken home with an alcoholic stepfather, was a challenge for the young man. While living in St. Maries, Idaho, Greg wrangled a plane ride with the famous barnstormer, Clyde Pangborn. Greg was 6 years old.

Boyington was constantly in trouble from the time he joined the Marines and went through flight training. He fought too much, drank too much, and was irresponsible with money and had marital problems. Boyington resigned his commission from the Marines and joined Claire Chennaultís Flying Tigers in China in an effort to earn more money.

When the U.S. entered World War II, Boyington rejoined the Marines. In 1943 he was given the job of putting together a squadron, which would later become known as "The Black Sheep." Boyington was shot down and captured by the Japanese in 1944. He remained a prisoner of war until the armistice was signed. When he returned home, Boyington, truly a "Black Sheep," was awarded the Medal of Honor

pappy boyington

NO BOUNDARIES

SHEEPFOLD
12" BLOCK

Fabric needed: Focus fabric, light, medium light, medium and dark.

A lap quilt that measures 38" x 50" is made using twelve blocks set three across and four down with a 1" finished framing border.

Yardage: Focus fabric – $^1/_2$ yard*   Light – $^1/_2$ yard
        Dark – $^1/_2$ yard (includes borders)   Medium light – $^1/_2$ yard
        Medium – $^1/_4$ yard

A large quilt measuring 78" x 90" uses 42 blocks set six across and seven down with a 3" finished framing border.

Yardage: Focus fabric – 1 $^1/_2$ yards*   Medium light – 1 $^1/_2$ yards
        Dark – 1 $^3/_4$ yards   Light – 1 $^1/_2$ yards
        Medium – $^3/_4$ yard

*Check your fabric and see how many motifs you can get from this yardage. You will be using a 6 $^1/_2$" square so the yardage is dependent upon spacing and repeats of the print.

Cutting instructions:

■ **From the focus fabric** – Cut 12 (42) 6 1/2" squares (Template C), being careful to cut around the area you want to appliqué to the outer edge of the block.

■ **From the light and medium light fabric** – Cut 4 (14) 3 1/2" strips across the width of each of the fabrics. Subcut the strips into 24 (84) 6 1/2" lengths or use template B.

■ **From the medium and dark fabrics** – Cut 2 (7) 3 1/2" strips from each of the fabrics. Subcut the strips into 24 (84) 3 1/2" squares (Template A). You should have a total of 48 squares.

NOTE: You will be making two different color ways of this block. By alternating the colors, each block will show up after being sewn together thereby creating a more interesting pattern.

Piecing instructions:

■ Sew a dark A square to a light B strip and add a medium A square to the other end. Make 12 (84) of these units.

■ Sew a dark A square to a medium light B strip and add a medium A square to the other end of the strip. Make 12 (84) of these units.

■ Sew a light B strip to the top and the bottom of the focus fabric square being careful to leave the area you want to appliqué to the outer edge of the block free. Make 21 blocks this coloration and 21 using the medium light strips at the top and bottom.

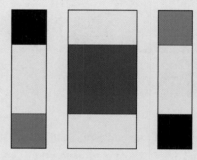

■ Add the two side units, placing the dark square to the upper corner on one side and the lower corner on the other side.

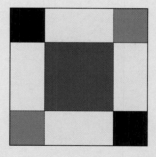

■ Make 6 (21) blocks using this coloration and 6 (21) using the other coloration.

■ Pull the portion of the block you want to emphasize out of the seam line and appliqué in place.

■ Sew the blocks together alternating the blocks made with the light strips and the blocks made with the medium light strips.

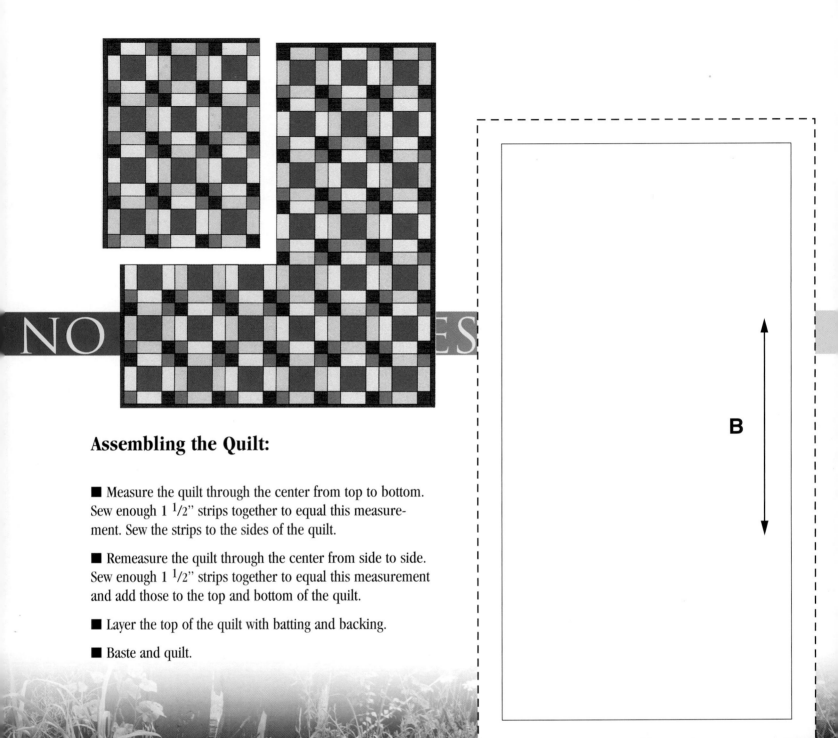

Assembling the Quilt:

■ Measure the quilt through the center from top to bottom. Sew enough 1 $^1/2$" strips together to equal this measurement. Sew the strips to the sides of the quilt.

■ Remeasure the quilt through the center from side to side. Sew enough 1 $^1/2$" strips together to equal this measurement and add those to the top and bottom of the quilt.

■ Layer the top of the quilt with batting and backing.

■ Baste and quilt.

B

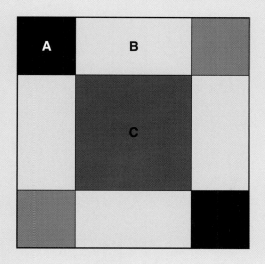

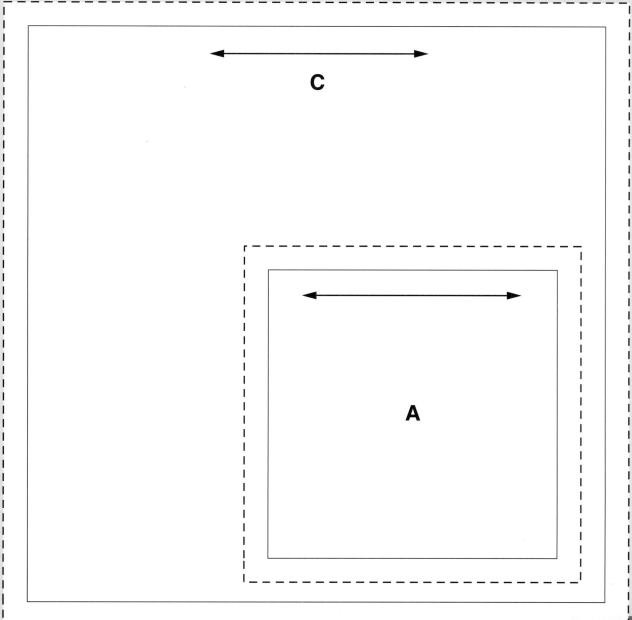

C

A

Judy Lovell of Independence, Missouri, pieced and appliquéd this wall quilt using the Square and Points pattern. The quilt was quilted by Nedra Forbes of Nedra Quilts, Liberty, Missouri.

SQUARE & *points*

courage

Here we are, 200 years later, celebrating Lewis and Clark's journey into unknown territory. Imagine what that must have been like. Their transportation was a keelboat and two smaller boats known as pirogues. There were forty-five people in the group and one dog. The travelers were enjoined by President Jefferson to map their journey, keep track of the peoples they met and the types of plants they found.

It took them three years to reach the ocean and cross land that would later become 11 different states. What courage it must have taken to step into those boats and not know how long the journey or what challenges would be faced.

Meriwether Lewis

lewis and clark

NO BOUNDARIES

SQUARE & POINTS
12" BLOCK

Fabric needed: Focus fabric, light, medium, medium dark and dark.

A wall quilt measuring 40" x 40" is comprised of nine blocks set three across and three down, and has a 2" finished framing border.

Yardage: Focus fabric – Approximately $1/2$ yard*
  Light – $1/2$ yard
  Medium – $1/4$ yard
  Medium dark – $1/4$ yard
  Dark – $1/2$ yard
  Border – $1/2$ yard

A large quilt measuring 88" x 100" is made up of 56 blocks set seven across and eight down, and has a 2" finished framing border.

Yardage: Focus fabric – Approximately 2 yards*
  Light – 2 $1/2$ yards
  Medium – 1 yard
  Medium dark – 1 yard
  Dark – 2 $1/2$ yards
  Border – $2/3$ yard

*Check your fabric and see how many motifs you can get from this yardage. You will be using a 6 $1/2$" square so the yardage is dependent upon spacing and repeat of the print.

SQUARE & POINTS

Cutting instructions:

■ **From the focus fabric** – Cut 9 (56) 6 $1/2$" squares (Template D), being careful to cut around the portion of the print you want to bring out of the seam line and emphasize.

■ **From the light fabric** – Cut 2 (12) 7 $1/4$" strips. Subcut the strips into 9 (56) 7 $1/4$" squares. Cut the squares from corner to corner twice, making 36 (224) B triangles. If you wish, use template B.

■ **From the medium fabric** – Cut 2 (10) 3 $1/2$" strips. Subcut the strips into 18 (112) 3 $1/2$" A squares.

■ **From the medium dark fabric** – Cut 2 (10) 3 $1/2$" strips. Subcut the strips into 18 (112) 3 $1/2$" A squares.

From the dark fabric – Cut 4 (23) 3 $7/8$" strips. Subcut the strips into 36 (224) 3 $7/8$" squares. Cut the squares from corner to corner at a 45 degree angle making 72 (448) C triangles.

Piecing instructions:

■ Sew a dark C triangle to either side of the light B triangles making flying geese units. You need 36 (224) flying geese.

■ Sew a flying geese unit to the top and bottom of the focus fabric D square being careful to skip over the portion of the print you want to bring out of the seam line. **NOTE: The flying geese will all point towards the center square.**

■ Sew a medium A square to one end of a flying geese unit and add a medium dark A square to the other end. Make 2 of these units per block, making sure the light part of the flying geese unit points toward the focus fabric.

■ Sew the side units to the center, again being careful to skip over the portion of the print you want to bring out of the seam line. You should have a medium A square on the opposing corners of the block and a medium dark square on the other two opposing corners.

■ To finish the block, appliqué the portions of the print you want to emphasize in place.

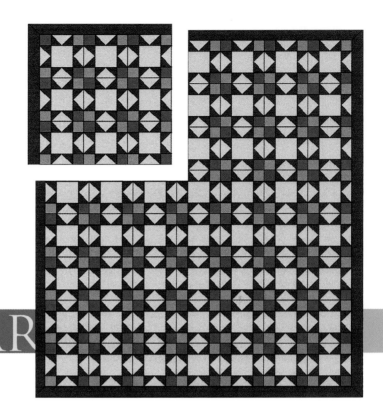

Assembling the Quilt:

■ Sew the blocks together.

■ Measure the quilt through the center of the quilt from top to bottom. Sew enough 2 $1/2$" strips together to equal this measurement. Sew the strips to the sides of the quilt.

■ Remeasure the quilt through the center from side to side. Sew enough strips together to equal this measurement and add those to the top and bottom of the quilt.

■ Layer the top of the quilt with batting and backing.

■ Baste and quilt.

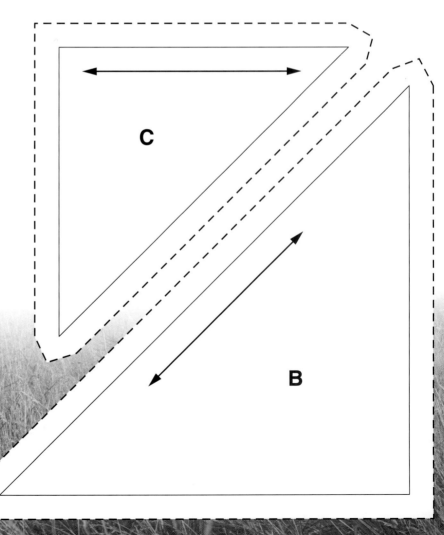

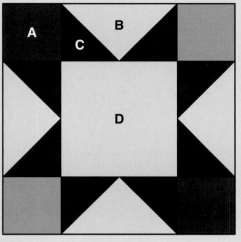

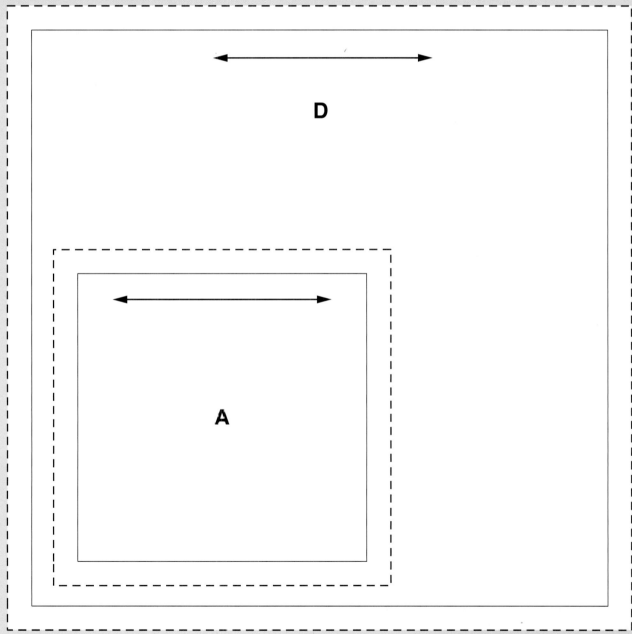

D

A

This Sun Rays wall hanging was pieced and appliquéd by Margaret Falen of Grain Valley, Missouri. The quilt was quilted by Nedra Forbes of Nedra Quilts, Liberty, Missouri.

Sun rays

compassion

Clara Barton arrived on the battle-fields of the Civil War like bright rays from the sun. Offering food and medical supplies to the wounded, she became the "Angel of the battlefield." Even when it put her own life in danger, she stayed with the wounded until they could be transported behind the battle lines.

In 1877, Clara Barton established the American Red Cross. Helping others through adversity was her mission in life. At the age of 82, she retired from the Red Cross after serving for 23 years.

clara barton

NO BOUNDARIES

SUN RAYS
12" BLOCK

Fabric needed: Focus fabric, light, medium and dark.

A small quilt measures 40" x 40" and is made of nine blocks. The blocks are set three across and three down and the quilt has a 2" finished framing border.

Yardage: Focus fabric – Approximately $1/2$ yard*

     Light – $3/4$ yard

     Medium – $3/4$ yard

     Dark – $3/4$ yard

     Add $1/3$ yard of your choice of color for the border.

A large quilt measures 76" x 88" and is made using 42 blocks. The blocks are set 6 across and 7 down and the quilt is framed using a 2" finished framing border.

Yardage: Focus fabric – Approximately 1 yard*

     Light – 2 $3/4$ yards

     Medium – 2 $3/4$ yards

     Dark – 2 $3/4$ yards

     Add $1/3$ yard of your choice of color for the border.

* Check your fabric and see how many motifs you can get from this yardage. You will be using 4 $1/2$" squares so the yardage is dependent upon spacing and repeat of the print.

Cutting instructions:

From the focus fabric – Cut 9 (42) 4 $\frac{1}{2}$" squares (Template A), being careful not to cut off the portion of the print you want to emphasize.

From the light fabric – Cut 36 (168) wedges, using template C and 36 (168) wedges using template Cr. If you fold your fabric, cutting through two layers at a time, you will automatically have the Cr pieces you need.

From the medium fabric – Cut 4 (19) 4 $\frac{1}{2}$" strips. Subcut each strip into 4 $\frac{1}{2}$" squares (Template A).

From the dark fabric – Cut 36 (168) wedges using template B.

From the border fabric – Cut 5 (9) 2 $\frac{1}{2}$" strips.

Piecing instructions:

Make 36 (168) units using the C, Cr and B pieces. Sew the C piece to B then add Cr.

To construct the block, sew an A square to either side of a wedge unit. Make two of these per block.

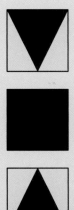

■ Now sew a C-B-Cr unit to the top and bottom of the square cut from the focus fabric. Remember to stop sewing when you come to a place you want to pull some of the print out of the seam line.

■ Add the two side units, again being cautious to skip over the print you want to emphasize.

■ Pull the portion of the print out of the seam line and appliqué in place to complete the block.

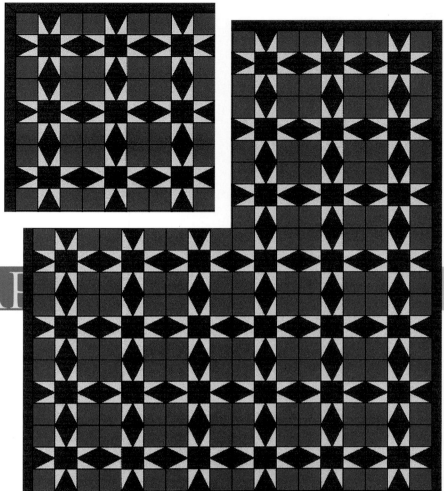

Assembling the Quilt:

■ Sew the blocks together.

■ Measure the quilt through the center from top to bottom. Add border strips to the sides to fit that measurement.

■ Now measure through the center and add border strips that equal that measurement.

■ Layer the top with batting and backing.

■ Baste and quilt.

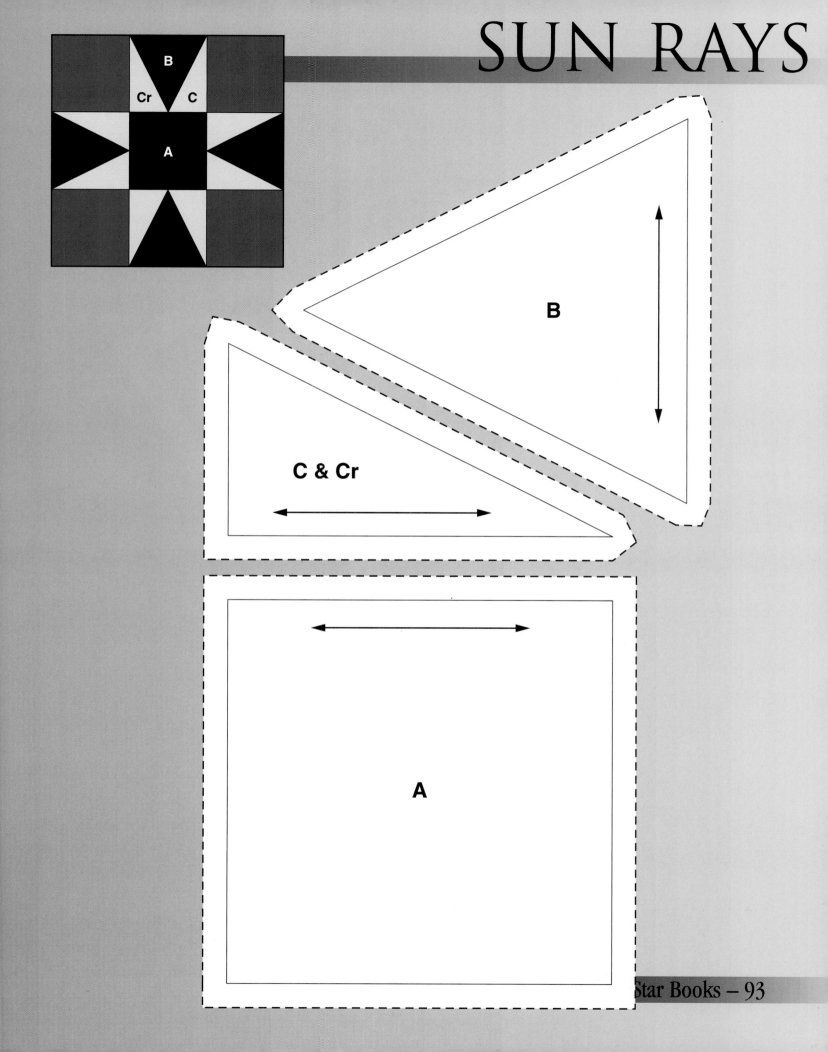

B

C & Cr

A

NO BOUNDARIES

This 4-block wall hanging was made using the "This and That" Kansas City Star pattern. It was pieced, appliquéd and quilted by Rita Briner, owner of Quilter's Station in Lee's Summit, Missouri.

THIS & *that*

spirit

Jane Addams, Susan B. Anthony, Amelia Bloomer, Elizabeth Cady Stanton, Julia Ward Howe, Lucy Stone, Sojourner Truth are just a few of the more well-known names of women suffragists. These women worked tirelessly for women's rights and the right to vote.

Even though some were arrested and fined, they continued on in their pursuit of justice for women. They all had a vision and were not about to let themselves be treated as less than persons simply because of their gender. No amount of ridicule could stop them. The boundaries men set for them were not allowed to contain them.

Women were granted the right to vote in the United States in 1920. The ladies in Kuwait were enfranchised in the year 2003.

jane addams

NO BOUNDARIES

THIS & THAT
12" BLOCK

Fabric needed: Focus fabric, light, medium and dark.

A lap quilt measuring 38" x 38" is made using nine blocks set three across and three down with a 1" finished framing border.

Yardage: Focus fabric – Approximately $^1/2$ yard* Dark fabric – $^1/2$ yard
   Light fabric – $^1/2$ yard   Border fabric – $^1/2$ yard
   Medium fabric – $^1/2$ yard

A large quilt measuring 74" x 86" uses 42 blocks set six across and seven down with a 1 finished framing border.

Yardage: Focus fabric – Approximately 1 1/2 yards* Dark fabric – 1 $^1/2$ yards
   Light fabric – 2 yards   Border fabric – 1 yard
   Medium fabric – 1 1/2 yards

*Check your fabric and see how many motifs you can get from this yardage. You will be using a 6 $^1/2$" square so the yardage is dependent upon spacing and repeats of the print.

Cutting instructions:

■ **From the focus fabric** – Cut 9 (42) 6 $^1/_2$" squares (Template C), being careful to cut around any portion of the print you want to appliqué to the outer edge of the block.

■ **From the light fabric** – Cut 2 (9) 7 $^3/_{16}$" strips. Subcut the strips into 9 (42) 7 $^3/_{16}$" squares. Cut each square from corner to corner twice. You will need 36 (168) triangles.

■ **From the medium and the dark fabric** – Cut 2 (7) 6 $^7/_8$" strips. Subcut the strips into 18 (21) 6 $^7/_8$" squares. Cut each square from corner to corner. You need 18 (84) dark triangles and 18 (84) medium triangles.

Piecing instructions:

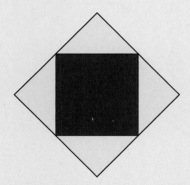

■ Sew the light B triangles to the center square, skipping over the portion of the print you want to bring out of the seam line.

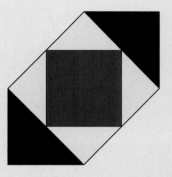

■ Add the dark A triangles to two opposing sides of the block.

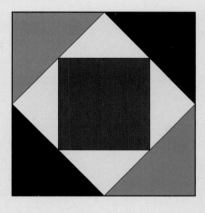

■ Add the two medium A triangles.

■ Pull the portion of the print you are emphasizing out of the seam line and appliqué in place.

Assembling the Quilt:

■ Sew the blocks together.

■ Measure the quilt through the center from top to bottom. Sew enough 1 $^1/_2$" strips together to equal this measurement. Sew the strips to the sides of the quilt.

■ Remeasure the quilt through the center from side to side. Sew enough strips together to equal this measurement and add those to the top and bottom of the quilt.

■ Layer the top of the quilt with batting and backing.

■ Baste and quilt.

A

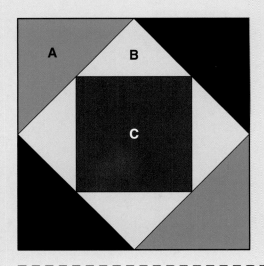

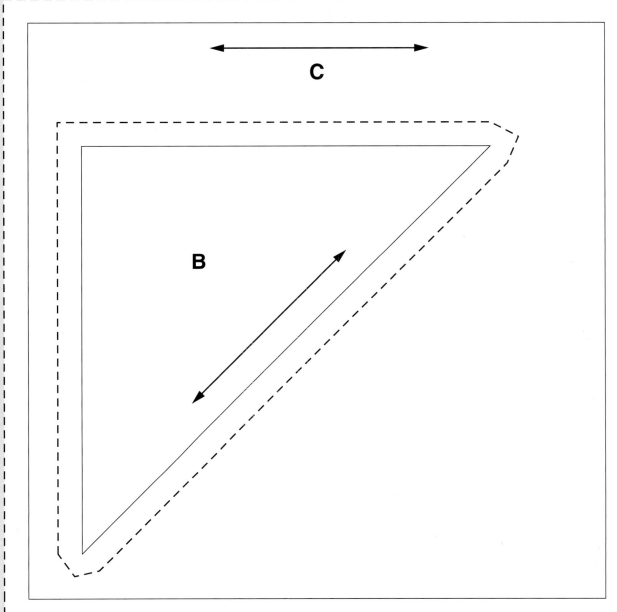

NO BOUNDARIES

This pillow uses the Cypress pattern. Judy Hill of Independence, Missouri, pieced and appliquéd the block. Edie McGinnis bordered the block and made it into the pillow.

CYPRESS *pillow*

■ To make a 16" pillow you will need:

> One 12" block
> Two 2 1/2" x 12 1/2" strips
> Two 2 1/2" x 16 1/2" strips
> Two rectangles cut 16 1/2" x 11" (pillow back)
> 16" pillow form

■ Make any 12" block. Sew a 2 1/2" x 12 1/2" strip to the top and to the bottom of the block. Then sew a 2 1/2" x 16 1/2" strip to the two remaining sides of the block. Quilt the pillow top after layering with batting and backing.

■ NOTE: Some people would not use a backing since this is a pillow. However, this top can easily be removed from the pillow form and laundered, so I recommend you use the backing.

■ Finish (hem) one 16 1/2" end of each of the two rectangles you cut for the back of the pillow.

■ Line up the outside edges of the pillow front with the right sides facing. The two hemmed portions of the rectangles should overlap each other. The top rectangle will overlap the bottom rectangle.

■ Sew all around the outside edges. Round off the corners as you are sewing. Turn right side out and insert the pillow form.

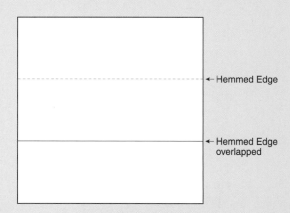

← Hemmed Edge

← Hemmed Edge overlapped

NO BOUNDARIES

The Crow's Nest table runner was made by Carol Christopher of Blue Springs, Missouri.

CROW'S NEST
table runner

This table runner, made by Carol Christopher of Blue Springs, Missouri, reminds you of lemons, limes and oranges. Isn't this a sunny addition for a dining room table? Carol used orange, lime green and lemon yellow batiks for her fabric.

■ It is made using four 12" Crow's Nest blocks and is sashed with 1 1/2" x 12" finished strips.

■ Bright cornerstones complete the sashing strips. The directions for making the blocks and sashing can be found on page 31.

Computer cover
designed and made
by Edie McGinnis,
Kansas City,
Missouri.

LAPTOP
computer cover

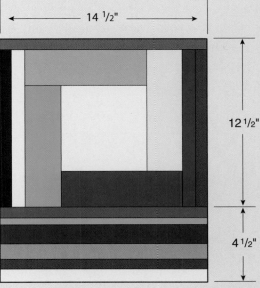

■ Measure the top of your computer. I have a Toshiba Laptop and it is 11 $^1/_2$" x 13 $^1/_2$" with a depth of 2" at the tallest point of the computer. The measurements of your computer may be different so take the time to measure.

■ Choose a block for the top. I picked the Bright Hopes Variation block which is fine as far as the height is concerned but not large enough for the width. Instead of cutting 3 $^1/_2$" strips to go around the center motif, cut 2 $^1/_2$" strips and make a 10 $^1/_2$" block. By making the smaller block, the whole top will look more balanced. Sew random width strips around the block. Of course, you need to sew either more strips or wider strips to the sides in order to end up with a rectangle.

■ After adding enough strips to get the rectangle the correct size (12 $^1/_2$" x 14 $^1/_2$" including seam allowances) begin sewing random width strips to the bottom of the rectangle. You want to make a flap to tuck into the bottom of the cover so add enough strips to increase the size of the rectangle by 4 $^1/_2$" on the bottom.

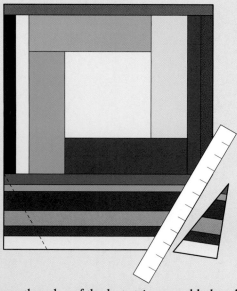

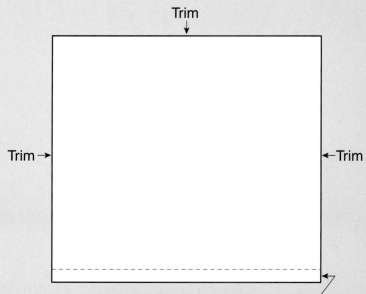

Trim

Trim →   ← Trim

Roll this edge toward the back and hem.

■ Place a ruler on the edge of the last strip you added to the bottom and cut at a 60 degree angle from the base of the flap area to the corner of the cover. Flip the ruler over and cut the other side of the flap in the same manner.

■ Using the piece you have just made as a pattern, cut a piece of batting and lining the same size. Layer the three pieces beginning with the batting. Place the computer cover top right side up on the batting. Place the lining on top of the cover with right sides facing. Start sewing the three layers together beginning at one corner of the flap and ending at the other corner of the flap. Turn it right side out. DO NOT SEW THE SIDES CLOSED AT THIS TIME! Pin the layers together and quilt the top on your sewing machine using your walking foot.

■ Cut a 13 $^1/_2$" x 15 $^1/_2$" rectangle of batting and lining for the bottom of the cover. Cut a rectangle of fabric for the bottom of the cover 14 $^1/_4$" x 15 $^1/_2$". This will be a larger piece than you actually need but it insures that you will have enough area no matter how tightly you quilt it. Layer the three pieces with the batting in the center with the right sides of the lining and back fabric facing away from the batting. Leave the excess fabric on the bottom piece hanging out toward the front of the cover. Quilt any design you wish onto this rectangle. After you have finished quilting, trim the rectangle to the same width as the top. Roll the extra fabric along the front edge back towards the lining and stitch in place. This will give the edge a finished look. Now trim the length of the rectangle from the unhemmed portion of the rectangle.

■ Now cut two 3" x 40 $^1/_2$" strips for the sides, one strip of fabric to match the top and one strip of lining. Cut one strip of batting 3" x 39 $^1/_2$". Layer the three strips together with the rights sides away from the batting. You should have an extra $^1/_2$" of the lining and outer fabric which will enable you to tuck the ends of the strips in towards the batting. Sew the strips to the top and bottom of the cover. If you have a serger, this is a great place to use it. If not, use an overcast stitch. Stitch the ends closed to finish the cover.

QUILT BOOKS
by The Kansas City Star

Star Quilts I: One Piece At A Time

Star Quilts II: More Kansas City Star Quilts

Star Quilts III: Outside the Box

Star Quilts IV: Prairie Flower: A Year On The Plains

Star Quilts V: The Sister Blocks

Star Quilts VI: Kansas City Quiltmakers

Star Quilts VII: O'Glory: Americana Quilt Blocks
    from The Kansas City Star

Star Quilts VIII: Hearts & Flowers: Hand Appliqué
    From Start to Finish

Star Quilts IX: Roads & Curves Ahead

Star Quilts X: Celebration of American Life: Appliqué Patterns
    Honoring a Nation and Its People

Star Quilts XI: Women of Grace & Charm: A Quilting Tribute to the
    Women Who Served in World War II

Star Quilts XII: A Heartland Album: More Techniques
    in Hand Appliqué

Star Quilts XIII: Quilting A Poem: Designs Inspired
    by America's Poets

Star Quilts XIV: Carolyn's Paper-Pieced Garden:
    Patterns for Miniature and Full-Sized Quilts

Star Quilts XV: Murders On Elderberry Road: Mystery Book

Star Quilts XVI: Friendships in Bloom: Round Robin Quilts

Star Quilts XVII: Baskets of Treasures: Designs Inspired
    by Life Along the River

Star Quilts XVIII: Heart & Home: Unique American Women
    and the Houses that Inspire

Star Quilts XIX : Women of Design

Star Quilts XX : The Basics : An Easy Guide to Beginning
    Quiltmaking

Star Quilts XXI : Four Block Quilts Echoes of History,
    Pieced Boldly & Appliquéd Freely

Project books:
    Santa's Parade of Nursery Rhymes
    Fan Quilt Memories: A Selection of Fan Quilts from
        The Kansas City Star

NOTES